Don't Be Invisible Be Fabulous
Volume 4

Awakening and Deepening to Truth

Compiled by

Dorris Burch

Don't Be Invisible Be Fabulous, Volume 4: Awakening and Deepening to Truth

Copyright © 2019 Dorris Burch

All rights reserved. No part of this book may be reproduced or transmitted in any form or by any means, electronic or mechanical, including photography, recording or any information storage and retrieval system without written permission from the authors and publisher.

Each author in this book retains the copyright and therefore all rights and subrights to her individual chapter, used herein with her permission. Each author is responsible for the individual opinions expressed and statements made.

Published by Fab Factor Publishing
Tinley Park, IL
www.thefabfactor.com

ISBN: 978-0-578-53033-8

Cover design, layout, and typesetting:
Fab Factor Publishing

Cover photo: Charles Taitt

For you....

Do what you're guided to do (if you think you don't know, think again, you always do, maybe you gotta listen more often, but start with doing what you'd do if you did know)

Do it without question, even if it makes no sense or seems not relevant to the thing you're trying to achieve

God is always there.

Flow is always there.

Power and knowledge and creativity and truth beyond the physical is always there.

Support is ALWAYS there.

Finally, because really this should be there the whole way through -

Believe.

Believe that all of this works, that it's real, that it's available for you and that it is of COURSE coming. Why would it not?

TABLE OF CONTENTS

INTRODUCTION 7

RECLAIM YOUR LIFE, ONE BITE AT A TIME
Dawn McGee 9

HOPE AND FAITH
Molly McGlynn Knoderer 29

BREAK FREE & REACH YOUR DREAMS
Kristi Heffelfinger 57

LOVE IS ETERNAL, AND SO ARE YOU
Maria Peth, PhD 81

RECONFIGURE YOUR COMPASS
Lori Ciaccio 99

JOURNEY TO UNSTOPPABLE
Jessica Mull 123

ACKNOWLEDGMENTS 163

AN INVITATION FROM DORRIS 165

MEET DORRIS BURCH 166

CONTACT 168

INTRODUCTION

The truth is that there are no limits. There is no such thing as too big/passionate/intense/fun/abundant for you.

Ask to be guided to people who get that. My awakening and deepening to truth moment was really letting go that I was suppose to be a corporate girl who battled to climb the ladder of success no matter how exhausting it is and wearing the mask to just be able to function in that environment. I spent those years in corporate world telling myself that I couldn't have my own business (and by default become the real ME) 'that' way. That people didn't want me to talk about THAT. That they wouldn't BUY something like that! That I wasn't THAT sort of woman with a voice and message, and that I just had to stick with what I knew and was good at, until 'one day'... One day, I suppose, being the day when I was known enough, accepted enough, had a big enough name. Really what I was telling myself was when I was GOOD enough. When I ALLOWED myself enough. When I finally gave myself PERMISSION enough to JUST BE ME AND LET THE WORLD SEE IT.

I created the fabulous Dorris Burch. She is the real me. She is who I was always meant to be. But I had to find her + let her out. How?... I got myself in the energy of the only person I knew at that time who's life + business reminded me of what I wanted + who I could be. I kept her in my ear and in my mind. Her lectures played in my living room. Her homework filled my journals. Her way of seeing life, helped me realize what was possible for me.

I have a message for you: The only way to set new standards, grow a business, change your life, is to... decide. That's it. Decide. There is no magic formula. There is only you getting honest, getting clear, trusting your heart/your desires/the guidance you receive. And deciding. Deciding it will shift. Deciding you will see it differently. I don't know where you are stuck in your life. Or where you feel under-supported. Or what kind of hot mess situations you sometimes create for yourself...

... but I can say this: You are enough. You are worthy. You are made for fabulousness. And your time is mother-effing now. Your time is now. Your time is now. Your time is now. You forgot how powerful you are. And things change (majorly) when you decide that you are no longer available for life at a certain standard. You have to change your mind first. Change. Your. Mind. Feel new feelings. Assume a new energy. And decide how this life thing will work for you. From there, you take any inspired action you are led to. If it feels good. If it feels like what you want to do. If it calls to you or moves you... you do it. It may feel scary, but underneath the fear... you know it's right. You know it is your next big, expansive step. With that in mind, **"Know the Truth, and the Truth shall make you free"** ~said by Jesus

Dorris Burch

RECLAIM YOUR LIFE, ONE BITE AT A TIME

I DID, AND SO CAN YOU!

Dawn McGee

Some of the biggest lessons I took away from my childhood were: Always live with integrity. Finish what you start. Treat others as you would like to be treated. Finish all the food on your plate.

LIKE ANY GREAT STORY, MINE BEGINS WITH...

Food. It stirs up memories and emotions in so many of

us. I grew up with lots of comfort food. In my house, dinner had to be meat and potatoes because that was just how it needed to be in my father's opinion. As for me, I was a starchy carb kind of kid. I loved everything about bread – the smell of fresh bread, the chewy goodness, the fresh challah rolls on Friday, fresh bagels with cream cheese, toast with butter when I wasn't feeling well. I think that growing up in a Jewish household, we really personified the concept of comfort food. We celebrated with food, we mourned with food, we socialized with food, we virtually planned our lives around food. It was foundational. To this day, I can't show up at someone's house without bringing some food or wine. It would be like showing up naked. Jewish holidays often had traditional dishes; my mom would make her stuffed cabbage and we'd always have fresh challah bread.

    Different holidays would have different foods that were a part of each. Rosh Hashanah (Jewish New Year) and Yom Kippur (Day of Atonement) are significant holidays in the Jewish religion and were particularly big food days. We always have apples and honey to represent a sweet new year. Rosh Hashanah was also filled with fresh challah, pot roast, stuffed cabbage, noodle kugel. Lots of heavy foods, tons of starchy stuff. We always feasted until we were full. My own Yom Kippur tradition has evolved over the years as my kiddo has grown up, but when I was growing up, we'd always go for a walk, to forget that we were fasting that day and we were hungry. Once our fast was over, we'd have a huge meal to celebrate breaking our fast. Eating was one of the few times that my family was sitting down together. Most of the time, we were in different directions – work, homework, friends, etc. Now, we are less indulgent, we tend to have a simple dinner, but the traditions are still important.

Now, for Yom Kippur, we take a walk down by the canal near our house with our leftover challah from Rosh Hashanah. Every year, we toss pieces of the challah into the canal to symbolize the habits, etc. that we want to get rid of for the coming year. Like, maybe we want to be more patient with each other. Or, be more patient with other drivers on the road. Or, maybe we want to take better care of ourselves, develop a stronger workout habit. Then, we talk about what we're grateful for and some goals we have for the coming year. It's a really nice family tradition that started when my kiddo was just 4 or 5. Even if this is the only time every year that we have deep conversations like this, it's worth it. Every year, I find new meaning in taking the time for self-reflection. Besides the major holidays, there was always a dinner or snacks whenever we socialized. After a funeral, while sitting shiva, the table was always filled with platters of food – deli meats, pickled herring, chopped liver. And dessert too. I loved the seven-layer cookies and the marzipan (still do!). Growing up like this, it becomes engrained in your life. I find it impossible to have people over without putting out some food and drinks.

As a child and young adult, I think food took on too high of a place in the hierarchy of my life. It was never enough to have just a little bit, I always had to have more. When the challah rolls came home on Friday, I didn't stop with just one, I'd have three. Instead of just one bagel, I'd have two. No-one ever told me to stop, I'm not sure exactly why, but I've always thought it had to do with my dad growing up during the Depression Era – there was never enough back then. So being chubby instead of skinny was a sign of health and wealth.

IT WASN'T LIKE I WAS THAT OVERWEIGHT

I was a chubby kid, and not terribly athletic. Not fat, but chubby. So despite being a fast runner, I was always picked last for teams in school. We never talked about how much to eat or my weight when I was growing up, but my mom tried to control my sweets intake as I got into my teenage years. Like most kids, when something is forbidden, it becomes far more interesting. And so it was that during Junior High, I would save my bus money by walking home. Instead, I'd spend it on a slice of pizza or a candy bar. Then during high school, my afterschool tutoring money helped feed a daily candy bar habit.

As you can tell, I never really learned how to eat to fuel my body. I ate because I was bored or upset, or it was mealtime, or because there was food out, or because I was told to clean my plate because "there were starving kids in Cambodia." My friends and I could never figure out how the kids in Cambodia would fare any worse if we didn't finish all our food, but it's something that all of our parents said. Whatever the reason, I grew up with the notion that leaving food on my plate was bad.

Since I didn't have a good foundation, when I went away to college, my eating habits only got worse! The dining halls were filled with sugary cereals and pasta and mashed potatoes and I didn't know how to figure out healthy options. Honestly, I didn't even know I was supposed to care about healthy options. I was too busy spreading my wings, making friends, learning. Plus, there were endless late-night pizzas, beer, and Chinese food runs. One of our favorite traditions was beer and wings on Thursdays – perfectly suited for college budgets – 10 cent wings and 50 cent drafts. Dozens of wings and many glasses of beer. By the time Thanksgiving rolled around, I was pretty much living in sweatpants and sweatshirts because none of the rest of my clothes fit. Needless to say, I came home with more than the 'freshman 15'. I probably gained about 25 pounds my freshman year. My mom had never been one to harp on my food intake or my size before, but this was different. She came home with info on "The Stewardess Diet", and that began my love/hate relationship with diets. The positive thing about the diet is that I lost the weight I gained and went back to school next year much lighter, and feeling more confident about myself. The bad thing is that I still didn't have the skills or education to keep the weight off and be healthy.

During college, many of us were in the same boat food wise, and we started to discover exercise. I started to play volleyball and run, and do some strength training. I found that in the short term, I could 'outrun my fork' and so maintained a reasonably healthy weight/size. Then my senior year, I tried out skiing and wrecked my knee, which lead to a long line of good news/bad news kind of stuff. I had torn my cartilage and had to have surgery. During rehab and over the next several years, I found that my knee felt better when the muscles around it were stronger and I was lighter. So, I began a regular workout habit and a long-term relationship with Weight Watchers.

I enjoyed going to the gym, there were a group of folks who were there every morning and it had a little community feel to it. I loved using the machines and weights and feeling myself growing stronger; it brought a greater sense of confidence to everything I did. Pretty soon, I was running five miles a day. My gym had a roof-top track, which made for a great view and wonderful sunrises. I loved fitting into my clothes better and running up the steps easier. I could go out dancing with my friends and not be exhausted at the end of the night – this was good! We would go out dancing most Thursday nights, with dinner beforehand. I figured out that I did not enjoy dancing on a full stomach, so I'd eat lightly – not stuffing myself, but just enough. Inch by inch, I was starting to put the puzzle pieces together.

THE GAP BETWEEN WHAT WE KNOW AND WHAT WE DON'T

And I started playing around with nutritional supplements – ginseng, super blue-green algae – things that promised more energy and easy weight loss. Eventually, I'd realize that there wasn't an 'easy button' when it comes to being healthy. It's not super hard either, but it takes knowledge. And here's the thing about knowing the right way to eat – once you know, you can choose to ignore it, but you can never un-know it.

Somewhere along the way, there was a Weight Watchers group in the building where I worked, so I joined. Seemed like the thing to do, and a good way to keep my weight under control. It felt like if I didn't pay excruciatingly close attention to the number on the scale, it would creep higher and higher. At the same time, it was an introduction into my interest in food and nutrition. The downside to Weight Watchers is that they don't give you any real education. I like to know how things work. After much trial and error, I figured out that if I had higher fiber foods and more protein, less starchy carbs, I could lose weight and still have a glass or two of wine each week; all within the bounds of the program. As I look back on this, I can see that I was starting to figure out how to eat for real. Eventually, I hit my goal weight and maintained it, becoming a Lifetime Weight Watchers member, but it still felt like I was on a diet and I hated that. It was so restrictive and I'm not good with restrictive. When I feel like I'm being boxed in by restrictions, the irritation starts to build and build until I feel so claustrophobic, I go in the complete opposite direction.

I'm amazed at my clients who can make small changes in their eating habits, who can gradually take one less bite of cake and leave the rest. I'm not the sort of person who can do that. If, for example, I eat too many buffalo wings when I order them, I have to stop eating them completely for a while and then I can come back to a moderate place.

Weight Watchers and I worked for a long time, but in the end, it just didn't give me what I needed. I hated feeling like I was always on a diet. It was isolating from the rest of my friends, who seemed to eat and drink whatever they wanted. Years passed and I limped along, following WW, but never really enjoying it.

Eventually, I became much more interested in the strength training world and on a whim, started training for a fitness competition. I worked with a trainer and we put together a plan. I worked out and dieted down and took a variety of supplements. Unfortunately, some of them were later banned for causing heart issues. Not a recipe for success. In the end, I decided not to compete when I realized how tiny the competition bikinis were. I just didn't want to be up on stage in one of those! ☺ On the positive side though, I continued developing my love of strength training and having muscles, even though it was still odd for a 'girl' to have muscles in those days.

Part of the training for a competition is 'dieting down' to dramatically reduce body fat and show your muscle definition during competition. Dieting down involved eating mostly protein and some fat (very, very little carbs) every 4 hours. My first introduction to a keto style diet. I had some great muscle definition, but it was not easy or fun to maintain that kind of diet and as soon as I stopped, I rebounded and retained fluid like it was going out of style. Puffy was not a good look for me. Plus, it was even more restrictive than other diets I had been on. No variety or fun flavors. Not for me!

So I went back to Weight Watchers because that was what I knew. I traveled a lot for work, so I needed a way to stay healthy and fit, but one that would still let me try the local cuisine wherever I went. I like to say that I 'travel by stomach', which is to say that I love to try local food, beer, wine wherever I go. Sometimes, my destinations are even based on them. One of my favorite spots in the country is Napa. I love to travel around and sample the local wines. And the restaurants! There is a real art to pairing foods with wine and it makes my heart sing when I find a great pairing. Over the years, I've been to vineyards around the world – Spain, Italy, Australia, Austria, Canada, and all over the US. It's so much fun learning about the wine-making process, sampling the wines, pairing food with them. There was a time when I thought that sommelier would be my best career, but the hours are pretty challenging in the restaurant business so I decided to keep it as a hobby. I did have a few years of fun doing in-home wine tastings, but that's a story for later.

Fast forward a few years and I was doing pretty well maintaining my weight with some sort of reasonable food intake, running and lots of volleyball. Which is when I met my husband. We were both down in the Caribbean for a 'volleyball vacation'. We got to hang out on the beach, playing volleyball with the pros and tons of new friends. It's kind of a funny story. I was going through a bad breakup and my best friend suggested I come along on this trip – she said her husband thought I'd like Mike. Turns out that what he really said was that
"Mike will probably like Dawn". And this is how the game of telephone is played. Well, we met and had fun and got engaged a year later.

Being an active couple, we were always out and about doing something – running, biking, volleyball. Which was tons of fun, but it didn't take long for my old knee injury to catch up with me. And this is where the saying "you can't outrun your fork" comes home to roost.

My active lifestyle was taking its toll. My knee was really bothering me and come to find out that the ACL was torn and my cartilage was wearing away, so the bones were rubbing together. It was super frustrating to be sidelined. I was used to being able to do whatever I wanted. So I had it repaired and started the rehab process. I couldn't go out to eat constantly and then run it off, but I didn't know any alternatives. I had still never learned how to eat to fuel my body; I was still just eating mindlessly. It was great that I did a lot of cycling as part of my rehab because that kept me fit, feeling good, my weight under control and kept me mobile. But this is more of the same old story, right? Using exercise as a way to overcome my lack of knowledge about how to eat.

Once my rehab was done and I had all the medications out of my system, we were ready to have a kiddo. Fortunately, we didn't have any issues getting pregnant, but unfortunately, I was one of those women who used her pregnancy as an excuse to eat 'everything'. Of course, I was feeling nauseous every day for the first few months, and it seemed like greasy, fried food was pretty much the only thing that made me feel better. And then peanut butter by the spoonful. It's amazing to me that my kiddo doesn't like peanut butter, he had so much of it in utero!

KEEP GOING UNTIL YOU SUCCEED

"I'll just lose it after the baby is born," is what I told myself. One of the many fibs we tell ourselves. Boy, I wish I hadn't done that! By the time Spencer was born, I had gained well over 60 pounds with my pregnancy.

Like everything else in his life, my kiddo came into the world in a hurry with an emergency C-section. Despite it, I set out to pick up my exercise where I left off, which of course, wasn't possible right away. When Spencer was just 5 weeks old, we did a 5k with him in the stroller. Ok, I wasn't really jogging, but I was walking fast and occasionally tossing a few jogging strides out there. I was really anxious for my baby weight to go away. Some portion of it went away pretty easily, but the rest… well…

We bought an elliptical for our basement gym so I could work out easily. I'd go out for walks and start to 'eat healthy' for a little bit of time, but I never stuck with it long enough. It was more tiring than I had expected it to be. I was up feeding my kiddo at all hours of the day and night, and it was taking everything I had to get enough sleep to function all day. Needless to say, the rollercoaster of non-sleep and hormones helped keep me stuck. I was just about ready to give up on losing the weight and buy bigger clothes, but that would have been admitting defeat, and that's just not in my DNA.

When Spencer was about 6, I was talking to a friend about my 'baby weight'. She bluntly told me that my 'baby' was 6 and it wasn't baby weight anymore. Was that my new reality? It wasn't the body I worked so hard for and it wasn't where I wanted to stay. But I wasn't moti vated to really go on a 'diet', and the approach I was trying of on again/off again healthy eating wasn't working.

Fortunately, it wasn't long after that when I started to get introduced to a better way of eating. I met my first line of bars and shakes. Our program involved having a shake for breakfast and lunch, a bar mid-morning and mid-afternoon, and a healthy dinner. I started right at Thanksgiving time and pretty quickly lost a good amount of weight. Unfortunately, because there really wasn't enough education or real food behind it, once I stopped having the shakes and bars, I gained back some of my weight.

In the meantime, I started showing the effects of hip dysplasia that I didn't even know I had. I tried a ton of different modalities to keep the pain at bay and get more flexibility in my hip – yoga, tapping, reiki, acupuncture, massage. They were all great and gave me temporary relief, but the damage in my joint was irreversible and it led to my first hip replacement. Rehab from that was easier than my ACL surgery, but still, no walk in the park. Fortunately, the next piece of my nutrition education came along and I learned about the science behind eating PFC very 3. It's super simple and changed everything for me. PFC every 3 just means that I'm eating protein, fat, and carbs every 3-4 hours. Portion sizes are so simple, we just use our hands. No more weighing and measuring for me! In just 8 weeks, I was able to make significant changes to my body – in shape and size and fitness. It resonated so much that I got my Nutrition Coach certification from Venice Nutrition.

Now, I had a career I was passionate about. People

would tell me that my eyes would light up when I would talk about nutrition. When we started kicking off our 8 Week Runs in earnest, I dove into the pilot group and was finally able to lose the weight I wanted to, eat real food, enjoy off plan meals, and not give up my glass of wine with dinner.

It's funny because growing up, my grandmother liked to read my cards to predict my future and she always said that I'd be a teacher. And now, I'm all about education – food education!

Later that year, life happened. Things took a turn when my husband was diagnosed with multiple myeloma and my kiddo had pneumonia at the same time. To say that things got crazy would be an understatement. If I wasn't at the oncologist or hospital with my husband, I was at the pediatrician with my son. Between their doctor's visits, trying to get my son to take nasty tasting medicine, my husband's chemo treatments, and his stem cell transplant, I was just trying to not panic or crawl into a ball in the corner. Thank goodness I had my health and my healthy habits. All of this didn't derail me entirely, but I certainly wasn't focused about being on plan. It was a full 6 months of just trying to survive at my household. Just as my husband was getting back to some semblance of normalcy, my other hip needed to be replaced. And that meant that my ability to exercise was pretty limited for the few months before due to pain. Then afterward, back into rehab mode.

You would think that would be the positive turning point, but the hip surgery just punctuated that fact that my knee was long overdue to be replaced. So, I scheduled my knee replacement for that December and threw myself a huge pity party over the summer. Which for me meant eating and drinking pretty much anything that was in front of me. Not a good thing. And unfortunately, that bad attitude carried into my rehab year. But I pulled out of it by mid-year and started to get focused again on my health. I did a full 8-week run and made some good progress towards my goals and started coaching others again. It felt good to get the feedback that the education and information I provided was helping people.

At the same time, I started to focus on how I could help others with their health, so I put together some classes on how to successfully navigate the Detox, Ignite and Thrive phases; as well as a workshop with general tips on clean eating; and a book called 365 Days of Healthy Living. As you can tell, I've never been one to tiptoe into things, I dive right into the deep end. Some may say that I take on too much, but I feel like there are so many people who need this message, that I can't sit still. I have so many projects that I want to get done so I can help more people.

Now I'm focused on working with busy moms who work full time and want to get their energy back and feel healthy again. From a business perspective, I'm poised to take my next leap forward. I'm eager to grow my Reclaim Your Life Movement based on my signature program – Reclaim Your Life, One Bite at a Time.

The core of it all is this:

I get it, I've been where you are.

I've tried all the crazy diets.

There's no silver bullet, it's about making choices and changes 1% at a time.

It's about setting a good example and being a good role model for your kids so they don't have to struggle like you are and I did.

This is not a 'diet' for a moment in time, this is for life

My underlying message is this – I was you – I didn't grow up exercising, didn't learn how to eat. I tried all the fad diets and then I figured out how to eat, move, and re-charge my body to keep it healthy. I got educated and now I'm here to help you so you don't make the same mistakes I did, and our kids won't make the same mistakes we did.

ACKNOWLEDGMENTS

First and foremost, to my family – my husband, Mike, and my son, Spencer, thank you! You are the reason why I started on my healthy living journey and why is it so important for me to be healthy – to be a good role model and to be able to be an active part of your lives.

Dorris Burch, thank you for creating this anthology and giving me a place to tell my story.

A great big hug to Mark Macdonald, the Venice Nutrition coaches, and everyone who lives PFC ever 3. Meeting Mark and becoming a coach was the starting point of a wonderful journey.

Finally, thank you to you, dear reader, who make a choice to pick up this book and read about my journey to a healthier life. Healthy living has a way of snowballing in the best way possible. The world will be a better place because of you.

Dawn McGee

As a certified and licensed IBNFC Nutrition Coach and a long-time foodie, Dawn focuses on both the health and joy of food as fuel for your body. She is a driving force in bringing education on healthy eating to more people through her community, 1:1 coaching, and her book "365 Days of Healthy Living." Dawn has been coaching clients since 2013. Prior to becoming a nutrition and fitness coach, she spent over 25 years in the high-tech industry.

She has been fortunate to have many opportunities to speak and educate audiences, and she truly understands the life of a busy professional. She also maintains a partnership with Jeunesse, a top-tier healthy aging company. As a Jeunesse distributor, she can offer you a variety of products to complement a healthy eating program.

Dawn has a delightful teenage son and a wonderfully supportive husband. Her son spends a lot of time studying karate and has earned both his black belt and first-degree black belt. Dawn's husband is a software engineer, and the

yin to her yang. Helping you plot a course to success with your health goals is what Dawn is all about. There's no dieting, no deprivation, and no giving up your glass of wine. :) Enjoy your food and love your life!

ABOUT MY BUSINESS

Dawn is an IBNFC licensed Nutrition Coach. She works with busy women around the world to rediscover their healthy selves - all in less time per day than it takes to grab a Starbucks.

Website
www.dawnmcgee.guru

Facebook Personal Page
https://www.facebook.com/DMNutritionCoach

Twitter
@ShapeUpBoston

Instagram
@dmnutrition

THANK YOU!

FREE GUIDE: Start your journey today – grab my free "Eat, Drink & Be Healthy Guide" at http://bit.ly/EatDrinkGuide

HOPE AND FAITH

Molly McGlynn Knoderer

What I am learning is life is really about finding peace within the journey. To have peace with the challenges (acceptance) and peace with successes (humility). It's about finding and learning to have peace with people who have had a presence in your past and peace in accepting new relationships in the future. And, for me, peace is found within hope and faith that all things in life will be.

Sometimes I don't know what I say to get myself into these situations but today I made a conscious, quick decision that is scaring the hell out of me and at the same time excites me because I just jumped into the deep end and forgot to put my water wingies on. Thank God I am a good swimmer, I know how to breathe and I know how to stay afloat even when it feels like everything is tugging on me to go down. I most always give in to the tug because I have always felt I am not worth the fight.

I'll be honest, this is so far outside my comfort zone but when I met Dorris Burch, the mastermind of this book, I felt a deep sense of trust and a need to participate. I don't know what I can contribute but hopefully, it's enough that someone can relate to the journey. I don't need to go into a full autobiography, no one needs to know my blood type but my life has been a journey with several falls and even more standing up. I try to keep my direction forward but know what has happened in the past has influenced the person I am today, for better or worse. I know what has happened in the past has influenced my insecurities as well as champion my victories.

I HAVE FALLEN A LOT

I have beaten myself mercilessly and am quite confident I am my own worst enemy. I have gone to therapy; hell, I am in therapy now and am constantly battling negative talk that holds me back from my true self. When I talked with Dorris, she saw me in a way I forgot to see myself. She called me out for hiding, hiding behind a story, hiding behind layers upon layers of fat, hiding from being authentic for myself. I will give you the shirt off my back but would never be so kind to myself. Over the years, I have come to believe I don't deserve my own kindness and certainly struggle receiving kindness from others; I question the intention and truthfulness of it. It's not the other person's fault, it's just what I have come to believe.

I am and have always been a dreamer. When I was a kid, I wanted to be the first female goalkeeper for the first ever Women's Olympic soccer team. At the time of my dream, that team did not exist but in my heart, I knew one day it would. When I was a teenager, I wanted to take over my dad's X-ray technician business; I wanted to keep and maintain a legacy and keep it in the family. When I was a teenager, I was known for my athletic ability, not academics. When I was 14 my uncle Phil told me he believed I was smart enough to be a chemical engineer but was too lazy and needed to study harder. He was the only person whoever believed in me on an intellectual level and saw that I was a dreamer who believed anything was possible. When I was a kid, I learned that women would never be on the soccer field for the Olympics and that my dream was ridiculous, I needed to move on from that. When I was a teenager, Ilearned that women did not belong out in the field managing and running my dad's business. I learned women weren't tough enough and I would never make…move on with that dream, it was ridiculous. When I shared that my uncle thought I could be a chemical engineer, I was laughed at and told that was a man's industry and the cards would be against me, besides, I was not good at math so what makes me think I could do that. Pick another occupation.

When I was in my mid-20's I was struggling financially and emotionally. I was sad and felt disconnected. I was starting to gain weight…oh, what I would give to be that weight again and was told I need to join a gym. I was told I need to work hard because no one would love me when I looked like I did. I was told my weight would interfere with anyone loving me and at that point I offi cially felt like shit and officially embraced that at no point in my life would I be loved and if someone told me they did, I did not believe them. I would believe it was a lie just to appease me...like all the other lies I was told growing up just to appease me. Don't get me wrong, I lived a very fortunate life; we had all the "things" people would want and more. When it came to having "stuff", we had it.

I GOT USED TO THINGS BEING GIVEN TO ME

Whether true or not, I am convinced I skated through high school because most of my coaches were also my teachers. If I did not perform well in school, I could not play on the field. I always passed my classes some way and I always played in every game. I really never needed to try and I learned how to get through the system without much effort or consequence. It was not until I was a student at UC Davis that I had reality thrown in my face; no money, no "thing" could get me through one of the greatest lessons and empowering moments of my life.

When I was 22, I was loving my experience at UC Davis; I had wonderful friends and slowly coming into my own. Socially, I was thriving...academically, I was failing hard but never shared that with anyone because I as embarrassed. I fell in love with Human Development, specifically related to aging and even more specific, dementia. I found my calling and was learning so much every day and fascinated by it all. But, the secret was, I was failing in all my classes. I can't remember how low it got but my grade average was below 2.0, I had received mostly C's and D's and knew the entire time I was hanging on by a thread. No one knew, not even my parents. I learned and I understood what was being taught in class but when it came to reading books and writing about what I was learning, I could not keep up.

Finally, in the spring of 1994, I got the dreaded letter from the dean of students that I was about to get kicked out of school if I did not get my grades up. I was baffled and I could not swing or throw my way out of it like I had done so many times in the past. I had to face up to the consequences. I went to my faculty advisor and for the first time as an adult asked for help. She knew I was learning and understood what was being taught because I spent a great amount in time in her office, learning from her as a mentor. She figured out I was memorizing everything learned in class but was not picking up all the extra work which required reading and writing. I am so lucky she was my advisor because she directed me to a psychologist who put me through a battery of tests that tested my auditory, visual, comprehension and reading skills. It was humiliating because I knew what she was going after (we studied that exact test in one of my classes) and I could not manipulate the results...something I became very good at over time. A couple of weeks after the testing and with my mom by my side, I learned not only did I have a learning disability; I read in a wave-like pattern and often mix up words/concepts but I also had a major comprehension deficit because of it. I was essentially told I did not know how to read. Imagine that!! At the age of 22, I did not know how to read…another dream shattered…another dream denied. I immediately heard, "maybe UC Davis isn't the school for you because of the quarter academic schedule, you can't keep up." Again, I heard it, "you can't…" Fuck!

There was no backup plan; there was no way I was going to start over and my ego, as much as it was shattered was not going to allow me to leave. What the hell do I do? With the support of my parents, I agreed to work with the psychologist to see if I could learn how to work with my disability rather than against. I had to be open to learn how to read all over again. I had to learn how to focus and block out distractions around me and in my head. It was more work than I was prepared for but I had to do something.

I spent weeks with the psychologist; I learned how to work with my disability and discovered from all the struggles I have experienced academically was also dealing with a great deal of anxiety and the anticipation of constant failure. I learned that while walking to school each day the best thing I could do was listen to John Denver and the Carpenters to help calm my nerves and get me focused; yes, John Denver and the Carpenters (I know I was the only student on campus listening to them daily… HA! HA!).

SO, I LEARNED TO FOCUS

I learned to block out distractions and I worked my ass off to learn how to read again. Not only was I reading successfully, but I was also understanding what I was reading and able to communicate what I was learning. It was an incredible feeling and I remember, for the first time EVER I was excited to learn. I stayed in school, I worked really hard. My professors accommodated me and allowed me to take exams in a quiet room away from my classmates and free of any distractions. It changed my world!!! Over time, my C's and D's went to A's and B's. I have no idea what my grade point average was when I graduated but know it was over 2.0!!! I graduated from UC Davis in the spring of 1995 and could not have been more proud and humbled. I learned how to learn and went into the real world with tools I worked hard for!

Even after graduating, I continued to read and loved it. I read for pleasure and I read to learn more. I was empowered!!! Over time and after reading through several books by Vietnamese Monk, Thich Nhat Hanh my self-awareness was growing, my curiosity was on fire and I felt confident I could learn more. So, without telling a soul (yes, I went back into hiding), I enrolled in a Master's program at the University of Phoenix. I could not do the traditional school model because I needed to work and felt this program would honor best what I needed. I did not do this for professional growth, in fact to this day, I often forget I have a Master's degree because it does not define who I am. What it does define is a level of confidence I often forget currently.

My Master's degree was an opportunity for me to prove what I could do and that I could learn. It was an awesome experience and after 2 years of hard work, I got my Master's in Organizational Development with a 4.0 grade average (I remembered that) as well as being nominated as my class representative throughout the program. I got to walk on stage in representation of my class to receive our diploma. I graduated!! I did it!! I earned it on my own. It was one of the proudest moments in my life. And, if it wasn't for me going through the journey of failing, standing back up, looking forward and learning to learn, I would have never given myself that opportunity. I would have skated through adulthood, cheating myself on growth.

I HEAR "YES"!

That journey of learning to read has really come to define my will and focus, two things I often forget are so strong within myself. When you hear "no" to your dreams as a kid, it does have an impact. For me, there are 2 things that have helped me work through or see through all the "no's" in my life. Really, it was not until I hit my 40's that I was able to put a label on what that perseverance was…simply and powerfully, it is Hope and Faith! I have always had hope in my life; I always have believed in the good and all things possible even in the face of "No!". As a kid, that gave me the label of stupid, naïve, blah, blah, blah…the list can go on. As an adult, it has made me become a dreamer, a doer, a visionary, a leader, a creative, maybe even eccentric; I have become all of those things because I have always been that but as an adult not only have I accepted those roles, I have embraced them. And now, as I dream what I dream and imagine what can and should be, I hear "Yes!".

I have always believed in other people, I love hearing dreams shared and seeing the excitement and passion pouring out of someone that shares their dream…maybe they are a dreamer but who am I to stop them! First of all, if someone shares a dream with you, you should feel honored that you get to hear it. Secondly, as crazy as an idea may sound there is rationale in the message and sometimes dreamers just need to say it out loud so we can start to adapt a vision into a reality. And, let's be honest, speaking as a dreamer…we always have some type of dream in front of us and it could be the next day we are on to something else.

It's because I have heard "No" so often that I don't want to be that person someone is writing about in 20-30 years that squashed her dream. Dreamers are creators, explorers; we are innovative and we are also off the wall. "No" is the fastest way to deflate a dream or an idea. I always wonder where my life would be if I believed in myself enough to push back on the naysayers. At the time in my life when these things happened, I was so impressionable and took what everyone said to heart…I did not believe in myself or even know myself well enough at that time.

With age comes the realization that you influence your direction. As an adult, you learn you can choose who your circle of influencers are. I must be honest, it's only been in the last year for me that I am understanding I don't have to be friends with everyone. It's not my job to make everyone happy and it's certainly not anyone's job to make me happy. I have always been a very social person with a big circle of friends...it's now that I realize that circle is made of mainly acquaintances and my real, true friends, while a small group are powerful! The make up of those friends has evolved into an amazing group of people who honor my dreams and truly listen to what my intent is. They understand I am always going to reach for the sky and stammer and stutter my way through those ideas.

THE EVOLUTION OF ME STARTED ABOUT 15 YEARS AGO

I moved to Southern California to open a new Senior Living community in Rancho Palos Verdes. It was an awesome opportunity and put me in a situation where I went by myself and for the first time was truly on my own. It was terrifying and empowering at the same time. It was also one of the loneliest times of my life. I did not fit into the "norm" of Southern California. It was there that I realized while I was confident, I relied heavily on others for happiness and direction. My two-year experience forced me to start being my own advocate, my own approval for my dreams and goals...not outside influence. After about a year of feeling sorry for myself, I started to take care of myself. I started making the most of where I was... I mean, who gets to go boogie boarding before work every day? How fortunate was I to walk down to the Pacific Ocean every day and walk along the coast listening to gray whales breathe as they surfaced on their trek North; how incredibly awesome.

I needed to redirect my purpose/vision within and knew enough that I asked for help and started seeing a nutritionist so I could learn how to take care of myself. I was learning to empower myself...I was learning to create my own path where it was only my approval that was needed. Of course, I always have a need to be validated but at this point in my life, I started to weigh others validation less and focus more on my own. This is such a crazy journey; here I am 15 years later and I am still going through these moments. Life is a freaking up and down roller coaster and sometimes I am holding on for dear life and other times I am screaming with joy with my hands up in the air enjoying the moment. That's life, right? Here I am 47 years old and I am finally learning this!!!

After two years and a lot of self-work. I realized I was feeling homesick and also incredibly empowered with this new-found self-awareness! That's the best high in the world...empowerment!! I headed back up to Northern California to familiar territory but a very different outlook. I had to make an effort not to fall back into old habits with people I already knew would not honor all the work I had been doing. I needed to find a new experience with my new vision and empowerment. I had a core group of friends that were aware of my journey and commitment to it; it was to them that I expressed want ing to meet new people, maybe, even meet someone who could become a partner on this crazy ride.

They listened and within months of me coming back to Northern California, I was introduced to this amazing person with the most beautiful, soulful eyes. After a short time and many adventures hiking, camping and laughing, I realized I met my soulmate and best friend. My world grew outside of myself when Charley and I moved in together and then shortly after, got married. I had to figure out how to welcome this new person who won my heart into my empowerment and confidence. I had to learn how to become a team. And, 11+ years later, here we are! He listens and giggles at my crazy ideas, secretly, I think he loves them because he sees and hears the joy I have when my brain explodes with ideas. I turned my focus in myself and put it all into him and to us. And, in this last year or so, I am giving myself permission to reintroduce empowerment and focus on myself, my growth and my development. I have my husbands support and I am ready to go. And, guess what this all comes back too…Hope and Faith! I have faith I can do this and to know I have the support of my best friend is awesome and so powerful. Right now, I am convincing myself that I can do this. Writing this reminds me just how powerful an experience I gave myself while in Southern California and it feels exciting and possible and totally empowering. And now, I have to get off my ass to do this!

This comes back to the people I am surrounding myself with. I feel like I am prepping my surroundings with people that will honor my focus and encourage me to follow my dream and participate in this journey rather than hold me back. All the holder-backers are slowly being eliminated from my circle and that makes me more powerful in my intent…Faith and hope.

IT'S THERE AND I AM READY

Taking a leap into a dream is scary and so exciting!! I work in senior care, have my entire professional career and since I got my Master's degree I always wanted to start my own consulting business; it's always been in the back of my mind. Working in Senior Care for over 20 years, I have seen too many changes and not necessarily for the better. I have seen the focus on service go from the residents/clients/patients to the investors. I became more vocal and disgusted with this changing priority. I think the climax of that disgust happened when an investor showed up to an Alzheimer's Care Community and spent 8 hours with me (the sales director), the executive director and the VP of operations from the company that managed my building (the same company the investor invested in). For 8 hours I was questioned about my marketing focus, lost opportunities and areas where improvements were needed. Not once did the investor ask to take a walk around the community to meet and observe how the residents were thriving in their environment or even that we had retired military, teachers, doctors, nurses and entrepreneurs who benefited from the great services provided; he wanted nothing to do with them. The investor wanted to know how I could make him more money because (he said with a finger pointed to my face), "it is your responsibility to put my son through college".

Me? What the fuck? Go fuck yourself asshole…my responsibility was ensuring the services I tell my families we can provide for their loved ones happens. My responsibility is to my residents and their quality of life. My responsibility is to my staff to ensure I get as much information about each resident prior to them moving in so we can proactively anticipate their needs and wants. At no point did I ever sign up to put this assholes son through college. Sadly, this became more of the norm and the expectations of me (being in sales) was more on keeping the investors happy rather than the people we serve happy. Over time, that took its toll on me and I was losing my passion for helping others and becoming more verbally combative when I was told to focus on the numbers rather than people. I learned long ago when the company takes care of the staff, the staff will care for the residents and the results are the residents are happy and driving in revenue to make the investors happy. Never once in that equation did it say to bypass the care of residents and staff for the sake of the investors. I knew in my heart the resident should always come first. Again, the trend in the industry was going away from what I believed in. But, I always believed we could do better. Which is exactly why I, with a dear and trusted friend, created my own company with a focus is on the serving our elders and their families.

DREAMS DON'T ALWAYS COME TRUE

The theme of this journey is hope and faith, two components that have become extremely important to walk through each day. This journey is a hard one, there is no road map without bumps, detours, and hazards but along the road is total beauty when you pay attention to where you are in the moment. Charley and I got engaged after 10 months because we just knew we were right together. We were also older and we both wanted to be parents; being old fashioned, we felt we should be married and a true family before we added any humans to the world. We agreed that after 6 months of being married, we'd try to start creating our family. Its something we talked about often and dreamed of becoming soccer and hockey parents, taking kids camping and introducing them to Mother Nature. We dreamed of teaching them about their heritage and watching them play with cousins, friends, and classmates. We had dreams for our future and in those first 2-3 years, those dreams included children. Well, we learned quickly (and without fully understanding), dreams do not always come true, no matter how hard you try.

After 6 months of trying, we had no success. Because of my age (36), we had to get my doctor involved and while she was very supportive and believed we could get pregnant naturally we discovered we had few things going against us…things we could not control (as much as we tried). My age was an issue; even more so, we learned I had polyps in my uterus…not just one or two but multiple. We did the proactive thing and had the polyps removed and waited. Sadly, within 3 months they came back. I was put on several medications, heavy doses of progesterone, 3 birth control pills a day for 3 months and heavy pain meds for severe cramping. We went through this for about 3 years…it was awful and tested us in every possible way. With so many medications and hormones, my personality was changing; I was becoming more angry, more aggressive and very reactive to everything (I was becoming a real bitch). I tested Charley's patience like no other. I tried to exercise more with the hopes I could calm my aggression down but it did not work. While I was not physically aggressive, I was verbally not nice. I became severely anemic and was losing all hope…I think it's safe to say I was becoming severely depressed. While this was happening in our home, I had to put on a happy face and be the cheerful, jolly (I hate that word) person everyone expected me to be. No one really knew the journey we were going through. Charley was my rock through all of it; he was totally focused on us even though I knew deep down he also struggled with our fading dream of starting a family. There were weekly visits to our OBGYN, weekly biopsies, frequent removal of polyps, medication changes, mood swings, exhaustion and tiny moments of hope that we could still have a child. As we went through each procedure to remove the polyps, we recognized they started coming back with more frequency. Our hope was slowly starting to fade and our faith that we could successfully get through this was also fading. We were becoming exhausted.

    I had another flare up and found myself back at the doctor. My regular doctor was not there this day and when I was told by an unfamiliar doctor that we had to do yet another biopsy, I refused. I refused profusely. I did not want to go through the pain again; Charley was not there and I found myself alone in a room with a doctor who would not listen to me. He performed the biopsy against my wishe. I felt so violated and unimportant in that moment. After the biopsy, I yelled at the nurse for allowing that to happen despite my protests. She listened but did not hear me as she went about her process of cleaning up the room. After she completed her tasks she left me in the room, still on the bed sobbing from exhaustion, stress and having absolutely no control over what happened to my body anymore. It was one of the worst experiences I have ever had. And, at that point, I was done.

I had to tell Charley what happened and, in the process, witnessed all the emotions behind it. He felt helpless as he could not be at every appointment (he was at 95% of them). The results of the latest biopsy came back with more polyps. Complete sadness. We needed to go somewhere so we hoped in the trailer and headed to our happy place near the Sierra Buttes. As we were setting up our site, I had another "flare up" (also known as bleeding profusely) and needed to stop. Charley was understandably frustrated and I got mad. He got mad. It was the first time we ever really got mad at one another. After things calmed down, I told him, "I can't do this anymore" referring to all the meds, mood swings, flare-ups, doctor visits…I hit my wall and I was done. I completely lost hope and faith. He supported me 100% knowing at that moment, we just agreed our chances of conceiving a child on our own was over. When we got back, I called my doctor and Charley and I told her we decided we were done. She talked about other opportunities/treatments we could try but also warned that with polyps increasing at such a rapid pace, I was now a prime candidate for uterine cancer. Cancer?

What the fuck of all fucks? I guess I blocked out the idea of cancer despite the multiple biopsies and follow-up phone calls letting me know I was cancer free. For me, this was never about cancer and it really never played into any decisions we ever made. Cancer…I am not getting cancer. With that, the discussion went from treatment alternatives straight to hysterectomy. It was time; we were done and so was my uterus.

Prior to my surgery, there was a great deal of mourning to go through. Our dream was literally being ripped out of me. We were going through this sad time privately; only a few people we were close to really knew what we were going through. Charley was my rock through the entire process and the realization that this impacts him as much as it does me was humbling to know a decision was being made on "us", not just me. It was a heavy burden and the guilt I experienced in being the one to deny him the opportunity to be a father was more than I can handle. And honestly, 7 years after my surgery I still feel guilty and sadness that our opportunity did not happen. To this day, I can't go to baby showers and tend to quietly disappear from friends who have had babies…I know it's totally selfish but it's also self-preservation. This was not just my journey, it was our journey as husband and wife. In the thick of it, it was hard and took a toll on both of us. Through this journey, it also made us stronger as a couple and strengthened our trust and faith in one another.
Charley was 100% present for me and I needed and wanted to do the same for him. It's through the love I could see in his eyes that my faith did not get destroyed; it was through him that while our journey would look

different from what we envisioned, I had hoped our life together would still have great meaning and love for one another.

One of my goals in this writing is to stop hiding or hiding as well as I know how to so I am going to be completely honest what this journey is like for a family that did not become what it hoped for. And, this is only my opinion based on what we went through, I am certain for the millions of families who have experienced this there are a million opinions/viewpoints. Here is mine... this time in our life, to this day is one of the most difficult experiences I have ever been through. When people ask me why we did not have kids, because they have observed what great parents we would have been, my canned response is, "because there is no womb at the inn." Most don't fully understand what I am saying and almost all won't ask me to explain (which is fine by me). I refuse to say, we did not want kids or "it just wasn't in the cards." I am honest, we went through hell and it sucked. It still sucks to this day and I still cry when I see my husband interact so lovingly with kids. It kills me that I could not give him something he so badly wanted...to this day. I'll never forget, just days before my surgery my cousin said to me as she walked out the door, "it's going to be okay, some people just aren't meant to have kids." That stings, it stings even more now because what the hell makes you the decider of that; it hurts to the core.

Don't make assumptions about people's journey. How the hell do they know? I for one think we would have been great parents, not perfect but that kid or kids would certainly get all of us. I hear people make comments all the time, "clearly they were not meant to have kids" without knowing the emotions and disappointment, stress, sadness, isolation, medical interventions people go through to have a kid. Not everyone is so fortunate to try once and boom, you're pregnant. This experience has taught me not to assume what other's journey is and to ask questions. Most people don't ask questions because they don't want to invest their interest and time in hearing a truthful answer…I truly believe that. I also know it's because some just don't know how to engage in that type of conversation. It's something I don't know I'll ever truly get over but it's something I know I have to move on from…that chapter is over.

But, be kind, don't assume and know there are more people than not who have had a difficult time having kids…please don't be so arrogant or entitled to think some are not meant to have kids when you yourself have kids…what makes you so special or better than any of those who struggle…really, tell me. Most people have no idea the depths of struggle we went through; I know there are people who have gone even further in their efforts with the same results. And, to those of us that weren't so fortunate…I would say, find your passion and share your love in that manner. I don't know what that necessarily looks like but for me it's putting my heart in my work. I love being with my clients and their families…they fascinate me and keep me curious about life, kind of how I imagine kids would have done for us. Your heart, compassion, view of life are of great value. Take the time you need to discover that and share it! Life does continue to move forward.

And, it does. We have created a fun life together and I am so proud of who we have become together as a couple. We are a team that will always have one another's back and talk through any battle that might come before us. We have already been through a great deal together and while we don't necessarily know what is ahead of us we know we will conquer it together.

Through this journey and hopefully to the last days of life, Hope and Faith have and will continue to push me and my vision forward. Every human has a journey; every human has a story of disappointments and triumphs. It's how we manage and manipulate those victories and defeats that truly creates the character that defines our own Legacy. I have a deep belief in the good of people. I believe people wake up each day with the intention to be the best versions of themselves. Some days we might be hitting all the high marks, accomplishing and pushing through the "checklist of life" and some days we are fortunate to get one thing done well (sometimes, just waking up is an accomplishment). What I have learned and will continue to learn is everyone gets the benefit of doubt until they prove otherwise. My therapist tells me often, "life is not easy and to be fully present there is going to be pain and celebrations." When I am struggling, I remember this and am encouraged to have hope that this moment will pass and my intentions (and incredible support system) will push forward. I am a person that has to process everything; usually internally because who wants to hear the roller coaster of thoughts running through my head. But, what I have learned is there are people who not only want to hear about the journey but want to participate in the journey as well.

In my 47 years, I am finally at a point in my life that I am surrounded by people who are willing to go for a ride with me and in turn, have welcomed me on their ride as well. The ride is hard and when lived fully present, it's incredible and rewarding and painful, scary, exciting, sad, thrilling, tearful and full of laughter. It is the essence of life and through faith that with each experience we become more alive. It's through the goodness of intention that hope creates dreams and opportunities. It's through faith that while everything does not work out as we hope, something better and more enlightening will follow. It's through faith that relationships blossom and bloom into a foundation that helps us stand stronger and taller. And, it's faith in knowing when we don't feel so strong and tall that we will get through whatever we are challenged with.

I don't believe in the concept of perfection and through my own journey I have learned that it's so important to support and be present for people who are trying to be the best version of themselves, even when they fall, there is still effort. I have also learned how important it is to be surrounded by people who are open to and want continued growth personally and professionally. I need to be around people who don't judge me for trying, for sharing ideas out loud and appreciate the need to explore and experiment because they know it's what I need for my own growth. I need to be with people who will laugh with me, not at me. I need to be with people who will be generous enough to allow me to do the same- for them. I will not be the person who judges and shuts down someone's dream, like what happened to me when I was younger. I learned and from that comes a gift I can now share with others…it all starts with hope and faith.

ACKNOWLEDGMENTS

I am grateful to acknowledge my parents, John and Jan and my sisters Jennifer and Kim for always being present in my life; you mean so much to me and I love you! To my aunts Lolly and Joan and my uncles Phil and Al for being great influences who encouraged my dreams (my aunt Joan is my greatest mentor in Elder Care; I will be forever grateful for her influence and support). To my friends who inspire me to be a better person, who encourage me to learn and grow everyday. To my business partner and dear friend, Deanna for helping me realize the dream of entrepreneurship so we can serve our community with dignity and respect; thank you for giving me the freedom to share my crazy, creative self. To my husband Charley, you are the light of my life. You honor, cherish and love me unconditionally; I am the most grateful woman in the world for our partnership and love the adventure of life we have created together. I honor your authenticity, your truth and beautiful soul. I love you.

Molly McGlynn Knoderer

Molly is born and raised in the San Francisco Bay Area and is a proud daughter, sister, wife, friend and business owner. Molly graduated from UC Davis with a degree in Human Development with a minor in Aging. In 2000 she obtained her Master's Degree in Organizational Management. Molly has worked in Senior Care for over 25 years and in 2016 launched Legacy Concierge Services with her friend and business partner, Deanna. Molly met and fell in love with her husband Charley in 2006 and were married in 2007. Together, they love to spend weekends camping with their 2 dogs, Barley and Murphy. Living in Sonoma County, they love spending time outdoors hiking, kayaking and enjoying mother nature. Molly is proud to be part of Polka Dot Powerhouse, where she met the creator of this book, Dorris Burch. PDP is a positive Women's Organization that encourages connection, unity and support.

ABOUT MY BUSINESS

In 2016, Legacy Concierge Services (LCS) was launched with Molly Knoderer and Deanna Shaat co-founding it in Petaluma, CA. LCS was launched with the vision to advocate, educate and empower families who are navigating the aging process with dignity and respect. We provide Care Coordination and Senior Living placement services. Backed up with over 40 years of combined Senior Care Service, Deanna and Molly offer comprehensive, personalized consultation and service for families throughout Northern California and beyond.

Website
www.LegacyConciergeServices.com

Facebook Personal Page
https://www.facebook.com/molly.knoderer

Instagram
https://www.instagram.com/mollyknoderer/

THANK YOU!

FREE CONSULTATION: If you'd like a free 30-minute phone or video consultation with Legacy Concierge Services, please visit our website at www.LegacyConciergeServices.com. We are grateful to be part of your journey.

BREAK FREE & REACH YOUR DREAMS

Kristi Heffelfinger

We all have a dream inside of us, what does your dream look like? Is your dream so big that it seems impossible? Do you often think about it, how it might look or manifest in your life or what miracle it might take to bring it to the truth? Yes, yes, and yes! Have the dreams faded as the doubts and insecurities have increased? I am here to tell you all that there is a hope and a future and even a miracle for each of those dreams and for each of you. Those dreams were placed in your heart before you were ever born and your creator is just waiting to see what you do with all that is inside of you! There are so many choices before each of us every day and with every decision an effect for the future and our dreams. What steps will you take today to bring you closer to your destiny?

DREAM OF BEING AN ICE-SKATING STAR

My journey was not so different as I set out to conquer the world. I had big dreams, greater than myself and more than I knew what to do with. My earliest dream was to be an ice-skating star and a skating coach. I began skating when I was 4 years old just before my fifth birthday. Skating became my life, my focus and my every thought. My passion and excitement pushed me forward each and every day. I started skating like most young girls, by signing up in group lessons. My Grandma Ruth gave it to me as a gift for my soon to be birthday. I picked up skating pretty well and moved quickly from group to group. Finally, I was told by one of the coaches I should be in private lessons. I still remember the moment I knew I had been chosen to move on to private lessons.

I felt so confident, happy and filled with excitement. I can smell the ice rink so crisp and clean. My little girl self knew at that exact moment, I am special, set apart, kinesthetically gifted. I truly was on top of the world! So, my journey continued and intensified. My daily life was not a normal kid's life as the years went by. My day consisted of getting up around 4am to prepare for skating three times a week; which meant going to bed early for sure. I remember helping out by getting the coffee ready for Mom, getting things in order and sometimes even putting the keys in the car and starting it. Then my Mom, younger sister and I would go off to the rink. I would skate for 2-3 hours; both freestyle and figures. I usually had a lesson with my coach and I practiced a lot.

When my skating session was over, I would change clothes, eat breakfast; which many times it ended up being in the car and then go directly to school. I would have a normal school day, walk home, do homework, have dinner, and get ready for bed. My life had so much structure and I pretty much knew what my days looked like; my schedule was full. I loved my schedule and the security it brought me. I always had security and comfort in that. Another thing I really loved was Sunday. This was a day that I went to Sunday school on the church bus. It was so fun; we sang songs all the way to church. I was invited by our neighbors and I have always been so thankful for that. It was because of their hearts to share that I had the opportunity to have a relationship with God.

I did not know how much this would help me and how much I would be able to count on this later in life. I would go skating at the rink for public sessions on the days I was not up early. I did this as much as possible and my mom would go do other things while I skated. This was my life and it was great! Things that I really did not do were birthday parties, sleepovers; I didn't have the time. The thing is I did not even care, I just loved to skate. I was able to go to competitions and compete quite a bit. This was really exciting and fun but also a lot of work. My mom made my outfits, I had new programs to learn and perfect and make my skates sparkly white. It was great! I really enjoyed performing in front of an audience. My most favorite program was improv; this is where you make it up as you go along to the music that they choose for you. This brought great freedom to me and a sense of accomplishment. It allowed me to express myself and make others happy.

My dreams both in my waking life and when I was sleeping involved me dreaming, envisioning, feeling and seeing myself skating… always skating. I would see myself doing all the moves I wanted to perfect; practicing the jumps and spins over, and over, again in my head. I could taste it, touch it, feel it, all of my senses were engaged. I was like a flower in a meadow flowing in the wind, free to be as I feel… as I am. I was so blessed to know and to have something so beautiful and amazing to know who I wanted to be at such a young age. I thank God that my parents were able to provide such an amazing life for me to experience. Skating equipped me for the challenges I would go through later in my life.

BEING A PERFECTIONIST

Skating did bring some things which were not so easy like always trying to be perfect. Perfection is a hard to accomplish, impossible actually! You see, there is a cost to achieve our dreams. The cost to have a coach, the expense of skating, the sacrifice of time and the need for parents to pay for it all. These things all had a tremendous toll on my family. If I had a rough day at the rink, I would be criticized by my coach, scolded by my mother and ridiculed by my dad. This made perfection necesary in my life.

This eight-year-old girl was being stretched and forced to prove herself and was constantly forced to justify her value. LOL! Being perfect... How does a little girl comprehend what that even means? That is not an easy or even possible, thing to do at any age. Being perfect created a little girl who was hard on herself. There was a learned behavior to act, look and perform a certain way and this was excepted always. It also created a false reality and unrealistic thinking as this mask of being perfect became who I was. This was something I had to break off in my adult life after I was married. So often this is the case we do not know how a situation will mold us and affect our future self. My journey has given me the tools to be properly equipped with what I needed to be a strong, amazing woman of God, a warrior, a fighter...the best me I can be!

    I am going to take a sidestep here for a minute and talk about perfection a little bit more. For me, things always had to be a certain way; my hair had to be just right, and I would do it as many times as it took to make it right. My clothes, shoes and overall outfit in general needed to look good but also feel great. I would try clothes on until a pile was sitting on my bed just to find the right outfit. As for my performance and practices, I would repeat a trick over and over until I got it perfected. One spill on my clothes I would go and change because it was no longer perfect in my eyes. Even when I would go camping, I would literally do my hair so many times just thinking about it makes me tired. I always looked good even camping. Camping was one of the only things I was able to do because I would water ski and that would keep me in shape while I was not skating. Always preparing for the next piece in my life.

It did not take long for me to realize after I got married that this whole perfectionist thing was devastating in trying to build a lasting relationship. I remember people calling to come over spontaneously and I would rush around the house cleaning everything until they arrived. This was a horrible experience; I was hot, sweaty, tired and ready for a nap. I was always busy thinking about, doing or getting ready to do a multitude of things. I have found it is a lot like planning a wedding. There are many tasks that must be done in a specific time frame and so much of the time there is so much to do, you feel as though you are on the verge of a breakdown. Always having things that look like they are in order makes it impossible to relax or slow down. It is as though you are always wearing a mask that says things are great, controlled and I am in charge!

On the inside, you are constantly reved up and ready to make the next move to keep the momentum going. Relaxing was a luxury and not something I did very often. What I knew how to do was work and get things done. I started working when I was a young girl, babysitting and by the time I was almost 14 I had landed my first job. Most of my life I had worked two to three jobs six to seven days a week. I grew up with words that were ingrained in my brain, 'You can not count on anyone but yourself!' I took on the world by myself and I aspired to conquer it! If I could do so well with ice-skating, then I could do anything! The only problem was the fortress that I had built up for my protection as a young girl. I found the fortress was holding me back from reaching my full potential and goals. The protection was safe and necessary as a child, but it created a plateau that was holding me back and took many years to understand why.

A new chapter in my life had unfolded when I found out I was pregnant with our first child. The gears in my brain began to rev up as I had thought of being the very best parent I could be. As I researched how to be the best parent ever...I realized if I did not get rid of being a perfectionist I would never be rested and I would not be available for my children because I would be too busy cleaning and preparing for everyone else. I slowly began to change the ways I thought about myself, about how others would think of me and then change my actions. As a perfectionist, I would never leave the house without makeup and my hair done, not even when I went to the gym. I always wanted outside approval because that it was, I knew as a young girl. The words of affirmation, you are so pretty; you are so talented and gifted. It just felt so good to hear and made me feel accepted and loved. I needed to love myself fully for who I was organically not with all the fluff. I started going out without makeup, being more casual, not worrying about what others thought of me and consciously relaxing.

The grueling journey started when our first child was born. Changing the way I thought and did things was like learning to walk again. Over time it became much easier and more natural to do. Making choices that I could handle like prioritizing the things I must do and letting go of what I did not have to do really helped to settle into a new routine. I chose to be present for my children and not worry about what my house looked like all the time. Let's face it, as a mom, you will clean at least 10 times a day and the house will still look like an earthquake just happened. This relieved so much stress, I did not have to be perfect. Wow! What a relief! My advice is to just be present, do what needs to be done of course but enjoy every day like it is your last.

You never know when things as you know it will change. Change… now that is a biggy! The thing is no one likes to change, but it is the one thing that will always stay the same. I remember my coach approaching my mom and me and sharing that he wanted to start training me for the Olympics. Another 'WOW!' moment in my life! How exciting! Finally, a change I could get behind! I thought I would explode I was so happy! What I did not know was everything was about to crash around me. I went from the top of the mountain to the bottom of the sea. The beautiful life I had been living was devastated by a title wave of circumstances. From training for the Olympics to my family being destroyed…the emptiness consumed me. My parents were separating!

My dreams to continue my aspirations as an ice skater took a complete halt when I was thirteen. My parent's decision to divorce changed my entire world. I was taking a break for the first time from skating. I stepped into a world that I did not know and that made no sense at all. It felt as though the whole world was closing in on me and I could not breathe. I was frozen inside; I could not move or think. I went from having a set schedule to this frozen place in time and not knowing what to do or where to go? At first, it was cool since I started skating, I had not taken a break and now I was going to take a break. Wait what? I could do those things that I had not been able to before. My only vacation I took was when my family went to Lake Shasta for two weeks and I could go because my coaches knew I would be waterskiing four times a day. Yes, my second love, waterskiing!

Since skating was my real focus, I did not really have a lot I wanted to do; sleep in, not having a plan or set schedule...kind of boring. I just did not know what to do with this freedom, for me it was torture. What I did not know, I would never be going back...not ever! This took me to a place of insecurity and despair. My heart was crushed, dreams crushed, and my world gone! The things I counted on daily, weekly, monthly were all gone! Instantly I did not know what to do with myself; brokenness was everywhere and my joy was gone. Have you ever experienced this feeling? Where the ground just came out from under you and you were just falling...This is where I was. Who was I? What will I do? Where is my security?

MY BROKEN WORLD

When I lost skating in my life, a part of me died! As I went day to day, my life was so different, so empty. I used to watch all of the skating events, competitions and it was so fun. After leaving I could hardly watch it at all. In fact, for the most part, it just made me cry, sad and I just wanted to push it away. I didn't skate a lot because of it. Something that brought such joy now brought me pain. As the years went by the desire to skate was less and less, the walls of protection built up more and more, I was in a safe fortress but completely cut off from the things I once loved. These revelations came over time, many years as I wondered why I reacted or felt a certain way about something. It is all connected in the end, and I now know why this story I am sharing today kept coming up repeatedly in my life. I not only needed to process what I went through, allow the healing to come in but also be willing to share it. I have learned that if something continues to come into your heart and mind, it is something to look at and process. This is your bodies way of making us aware of things. They will never go away until those things are dealt with.

How do I pick up from this moment, from knowing who you are and where you're going to knowing nothing at all? Is it better to have not known at all because this felt horrible, stuck, frozen in time...? Frozen in a place where I did not have a clue what to do with my time, life or anything else for that matter. Turning around to see the other side of my life, my parents; what I knew there also gone. In a blink of an eye it was all gone, the stable, consistent life I knew and loved, all gone! What do you do? You pick yourself up off the ground and you figure out how to live a new way. Somehow having faith in God made me think I was somewhat invincible. I should be able to handle all that comes my way and that if my faith was strong enough the problems would be fixed.

That is not the case. Prayer is one step, taking steps to work through things is another. It was good to talk things out. I did this with friends and at times with a counselor. The healing will come in the end.

Picking yourself up...so it sounds pretty easy right. Kind of like when you fall down, you just get up and that is it. Not really. Anyone who has tumbled like knows it feels like you have been pushed off a cliff and you are still falling. During the falling, spinning, fear, you can not breathe, and you are trying to see and figure out life. I can tell you at this point I just built up a huge wall around myself but especially around my heart. I had made a vow (a very unhealthy one) that I would never feel like this again. I would never let my heart feel this pain again, let anyone have power like that in my life. At this point I really did not have much feeling, I pushed that down as far as I could. In fact, if you would have asked me about my Dad leaving etc. I could feel nothing really, numbness mostly. The next years in my teens were intense and know that my choices were not good ones but I am grateful I got through them. The thing is I did not even know why I was making those choices. It was because of all the hurt, fear and the unknown. I thank my Mom for hanging in there with me when I know she was at her wits end with me and God for keeping me safe!

Before the separation, we had moved from our familiar home to a new home. It was a beautiful home on the hill in Hayward. We loved it! What I did not have now were my lifelong friends, my church, my comfort. These familiar things are needed for any young girl needs and without it is like being at sea without a compass. After my parent's separation, I soon settled into a routine of helping around the house which really helped mom out and kept harmony in our home. With Dad gone my Mom had to work three jobs and it actually really sucked! I was use to

Mom being around a lot and now she just wasn't. I did a lot of the cooking, cleaning and watching my younger sister now which kept me active and focused. It was a routine but one that was not creative or fun. It felt like I had grown up over night. With our mom and dad gone a lot it created a deep abandonment within me and my sister. We went from both parents around to very little time with Mom and almost none with Dad. Sure, Dad always meant well but he had his own business and always seemed to have things come up when he would schedule time with us.

I remember waiting with my sister and he would never come. Of course, there was always something that came up but as a kid how do you take that in? It only created thoughts like; I must not be important, not good enough, what was I doing wrong, makes you want to become perfect, you become hopeless, and feel abandoned. This created more pushing of my emotions, down, down, down and this was my coping mechanism, my protection of the little girl inside of me never getting hurt like this again. This was a very safe thing for me to do in a situation like this but I have learned that as an adult it has to be taken care of because if not there will always be a part of you that will not allow you to fully engage in life as you should. Another very key thing that I used as a tool was a Bible that my parents had given me for a birthday before they separated. The years in church has taught me to read the bible and I learned a lot. What I didn't know was how invaluable this would be to me and my future. In the emptiness, loss, and struggles that I faced my peace came from an inner knowing to read my Bible. Every time I felt bad, hopeless, angry or unhappy, I would read my Bible. All I wanted and all I prayed for was to be happy...As I prayed these words and read my Bible, I felt better and it became a habit because I knew it worked. I found God brought me guidance, peace, and comfort in a time of turmoil.

BEAUTY FOR ASHES

So much had changed after the divorce, but it becomes the new normal. My parent's relationship before all the changes was ok. We saw my Mom daily, she worked at home for my Dad's construction business. Dad worked a lot from what I remember except for the winter time or rainy season, he was home more. We were pretty fortunate to have our parents around so much. As a kid I saw them as happy, spending some time together, vacations, family time; it all seemed normal. I do not remember them arguing in front of us and that was a very healthy thing. When it all happened, it was somewhat shocking for us. I share this to give you an idea of what our perspective was as kids in the situation. Fast forward to after the separation and finally the divorce; things were completely different. Walls for my sister and I began to go up around us the more times of disappointment, the more walls and the deeper our feelings were pushed down. This went on into our adult life and eventually the times we spoke or saw each other were farther and farther apart. Our regular contact was about one time a year and then it went to one time in two years. We both felt as though he had died a long time ago and had given up on having what we felt that others have with their dad's in a relationship.

Honstly, I didn't even know what a healthy relationship looked like. My normal became no contact, no expectations and no real hope of change. The pain was so deep, it hurt so bad not having Dad around. I know that is what I looked for constantly, someone to just love me for who I was, as I was, unconditionally. I did pray for my Dad, that he would find what he was seeking, and God would bless him and that one day he would see what we had gone through and be remorseful.

My Dad came around for each of my kid's births but that was pretty much it. My kids do not really know him at all. Much of their lives they knew he was my Dad and Grandpa but they did not understand why he was not like their other grandparents. In that I mean the kind of grandparents that are there for you, call, set up a time to go do fun things, have sleepovers...you know doing the fun things that parents cannot always do. This caused me to set up strong boundaries for with my kids and I. I did not want them to be hurt or affected by what he was doing or by the inconsistency of his actions. Kids need to have consistency, especially with people. All I knew was what I had learned through books, classes, and teachings; boundaries are healthy and protect you. This was a great way to still have grandpa in their lives but under my rules of protection for them. As the years went by, I realized the importance of a daughter having a relationship with her Dad and basically having one around. Knowing what losing someone feels like now, I can honestly say it feels like a death of a loved one when you lose an important person in your life. With this type of loss, there is a grieving process and the beginning of understanding what I went through with my parent's divorce. I was hurt, angry, frustrated, hopeless, lost and fo sure wondering what I was to do with my life. With these feelings come the building blocks to that fortress or wall I shared earlier which included unworthiness, not being good enough, unwanted, abandoned and longing for a strong Dad like figure. This is just not the truth, but it is what happens inside of your head and then your heart. That was a huge revelation!

Renew your mind and the truth will set you free! I read this in my Bible and now it because real and truly begins to unleash my prayers to be happy. With this information I began to proclaim truth over myself, speaking it. Over time I began to see the fortresses being torn down and this area brought down and to rest. No more lies trying to break me down and keeping me from reaching my dreams and destiny or from healthy relationships. When I lost my Dad, he was dead and buried but this brought life back in my heart. A part of my heart that was gone was brought back to life as I stepped into this place of healing and newness.

The thing is that I still did not have a relationship with my Dad. I mean we talked to each other one time a year or even at times one time every two years. That surely doesn't make a relationship and not a close one. I didn't have an expectation I thought that was what it would be. In my heart, the conversation was much different and those words said I wanted to know why we were abandoned, left out, etc. It was another thing I just buried and left for dead.

It was a cold winter evening and I had decided to try out a new bible study. I sat down with high expecta tions of what I would be learning and growing with this study. As the video was started and the speaker was sharing about all the crazy things God was doing in her family; I knew as soon as I heard those words the same was going to happen to me. I was not excited about this, in fact, it scared the crap out of me. Before I left that night, I knew it was all about my Dad and by the time I got to my car I knew I needed to tell my sister what was coming. She was not going to like it at all. I called her and told her that I really felt Dad was going to contact us and to be ready. I also told her this door would not be open to us for long and if we did not walk through it, it may never open again. Before I even got home my sister had called me back and said Dad had tried to call her. Fear took over and she would not answer the call.

I knew I was next and sure enough in the next day or so he called me but I answered. It had been at least two years since we had talked and he spoke as if it was just yesterday. He wanted to connect which was great only I needed to know why. He felt a void and wanted to connect again. I had a lot of stipulations like if we let you in and you disconnect, that is it, I am done. I agreed to get my sister onboard and we were going to meet him together at a coffee place. I told God if I did not see remorse for the way he had treated us I was walking out and I needed to know his heart was in the right place. Let me tell you I was scared and all those emotions I shared earlier were all rising. By the time we were meeting, and I was driving to our destination I thought I was going to throw up, I almost pulled over. What that made me realize is how much was inside and how important it was for me to resolve these feelings no matter the outcome. My sister and I did a lot of praying prior to our meeting and were ready for the outcome. What happened was a miracle, truly. We both were able to share all of our hurts and ask those questions we had all of our life because it was now over 30 years since the divorce.

We asked if he ever thought about what we were both going through, how it hurt us, that we felt abandoned, struggled with our self worth, and fears. I asked if he realized how important it was to daughters to have a father in their lives and I had read that it was so important. He had no idea or the things we had gone through, the hurts we carried or the brokenness inside. As we sat in Starbucks coffee shop for over 4 hours talking about all of this, there was a moment where his eyes were opened. He began to cry and I could see the remorse in his eyes; my prayers were answered and my heart was touched. There were many tears from all of us and there was so much healing done in our hearts. I actually felt a huge bandage with healing properties being placed on our hearts, there was closure. I felt complete and closure with so much gratefulness. I was overjoyed with emotions and they were all good! I am thankful for being able to have a relationship with my Dad today. Brokenness restored and my buried dream of having my Dad in my life restored. Grateful!

What does our relationship look like today with our Dad? Well, it is better for sure but it is not perfect. I do not have expectations of what it will look like, although I do always pray for the best it can be. I just know how amazing it is to feel free from the brokenness, fears, aban donment of the past in all of this. I have thanked my Dad because of what I went through with the divorce, not having a Dad around made me want something more.

My intention when I got married was to fight with everything, I had in me to make it the best it could be, never to give up and always work on myself first. If I had not walked through this I would have never known the importance of doing what I could to have a strong marriage, and as our vows said through sickness & health, good and bad...fight, love, grow, compromise, forgive and do it 70x7 times forever! Did I mention it takes two...both people in marriage need to participate and give 150%. There are times that a person will have to walk away; abuse both mental and physical are just a few examples. You must always take care of yourself and if someone or something in a relationship is taking you down, ask for help and really search for what is healthy and good for you. No one deserves to be treated poorly, put down, not taken care of. My marriage today is better than it has ever been. Nothing is perfect, not any marriage, not even ours and knowing that it is a constant battle to fight for forever but that is so worth it in the end.

THEN YOU REALIZE THERE IS SO MUCH MORE TO THE JOURNEY

Back to those broken dreams, how do we see them come forth? By never giving up, always pressing in, asking questions, finding balance, working on yourself and be ing open to change and not connected to how things might actually happen. For me, it was after being married and having my third child. Skating was not really in my life. In fact, it took years for me to even watch ice skating without crying, I use to love watching it. My husband knew how much I loved to skate and although I didn't do it often it still felt amazing.

One day my husband comes home and tells me that I needed to go get a job as an ice-skating coach. I thought he had lost his mind, really lost it. There is no way you walk into a rink and say I want to teach and by the way, I haven't skated regularly since I was like thirteen. Besides the fact that I was working part-time at a salon doing hair and had three children to take care of who were now 1, 3, 5 years old. I had a full plate already. He would not let this go for the next 2 days and I finally told him I would call and ask. This meant I actually had to call and talk to someone. I was walking around our house one day and I felt this pulling to call the rink now! The thought would not leave me...CALL NOW!!!

I just did it and to my surprise, I was connected with the manager who I happened to have skated with. She remembered me and told me I was hired and she would share all that I needed to do the lessons. This was my dream; you know the one that I had buried and I thought was dead! It was here brought back to life; I was a coach! I can't express the joy that my heart felt that day! I taught with all my heart and was so touched by the experience I received and it all happened because I listened to my husband and my heart. I listened to the still small voice inside pushing me to just do it! We all have this inside of us!

Take a chance and listen to what you are trying to tell yourself and just do it! What do you have to lose? Nothing! You do have everything to gain! Do it afraid if you have to but you never know the amazing outcome you will receive...I dare you!

All in all, there are so many stories I could share with you about how things completely turned around in my life but that is for another time, another book. One huge thing I will share is how my marriage has been completely restored. My fight to seek wholeness, working on myself, trusting God, allowing transformation to happen in my life and being focused and willing to change has created an amazing outcome for both of us. I am seeking opportunities to speak and share my story so that I can help others with bringing hope to their dreams and restoration to their relationships.

Lastly, our realities as a child or truth as we see it can be so different than the reality of truth that really is so. My realities were all lies which kept me captive and caused me to have a hard time trusting people even God which kept me more secluded. I have had to reassure the little girl inside of me, it will be ok. When you go through trials that affect you like this, you must come to terms with things in life when it has all crumbled before you. Through it all God showed me He is my Father who I can always trust. My heart is healed from all the hurt and now I have a brand-new heart, full of joy, gratefulness, and happiness to share with all. My prayer is that each of you will receive all that you need in your situations!

ACKNOWLEDGMENTS

I want to thank my God for allowing me to learn all that I have through out my life. Thank you to my husband, my kids & family, and my friends for supporting & believing in me always.

Kristi Heffelfinger

I am a loving wife of 31 years & mother of three and grandmother of two. My journey in life has been filled with peaks and valleys but what I have learned is worth it all. My passion and heart is to share what I know with all of you to hopefully make your journey a much easier one. I love bringing transformation to people from the outside in. May my story change your life, mind or path as you take a piece of my sharing for yourself.

ABOUT MY BUSINESS

I started out as a hairstylist and now over 25 years later it has become so much more. I have partnered with Rodan + Fields skincare to help make a difference with single moms through local charity's; giving back a % of sales. My most important lesson is to always listen to others and listen to the inner voice within. Be the change you want to see happen and always be a positive person to all. I am stepping into a new place as I have began a journey to spread my story through writing and speaking engagements, as I am making a difference in this world.

Website
https://transformationbykristi.com/

Facebook Personal Page
Kristi Heffelfinger @ hair by Kristi Heffelfinger

Instagram
Kristi_heffelfinger

THANK YOU!

FREE STRATEGY SESSION: Thank you for taking the time to be a part of my journey. Please connect with me on my website for a free strategy session. https://transformationbykristi.com/

LOVE IS ETERNAL, AND SO ARE YOU

Maria Peth, PhD.

Personal truth is a powerful signature, an authentic and unique autograph of self-expression, freedom, and individuation. With each courageous step we take toward our genuine state of being, we uncover our distinct brilliance and the certainty about who we are. If there is one thing I know to be true regarding life, it is that we are endlessly offered new opportunities for self-discovery and personal growth, however we don't always realize it and sometimes it takes a while before we wake up to a better way.

How often have you asked yourself, *"Am I on the right track?"* or more specifically, *"What is the purpose of my life?"* Answers to these questions are not simple, for life is a process of personal discovery and design. Sometimes we discover our truth by way of an unexpected challenge or an issue that will not go away. Such as spending years battling a demanding dead-end job, or being deeply depressed in a loveless marriage? All the while running in the same old tired rut without truly being conscious of *"why"* we do what we do, or *"how"* to breakout of the runnel. I have discovered the way out of these shackles begins when we recognize the staleness of the endless rut, and are therefore finally ready to break free. Each of us is completely responsible for the direction of our life and when we awaken to the misery we are playing in, then real change can occur and a deeper understanding of who we really are and what we want awakens within us.

BE OPEN TO THE WHISPER

On my journey as a spiritual teacher and soul coach, it has been my pleasure to support thousands of people to a deeper realization of their own existence. However, just like everyone else, I too battled my share of demanding life issues, jobs, and relationships on my way to awakening to purpose, and defining my strengths and how that might manifest in the world. I stumbled through various professions on my way to becoming an author and angel expert. All avenues on my journey served as perfect life lessons to strengthen my character, and have led me to understand what is most important, in life and to actualize my truth.

I graduated from the University of Iowa with a

Bachelor of Science and teaching endorsement. The love of my life was offered a graduate assistant position at the University of Denver, so naturally, we got married and moved to Colorado. My first real work out of college was as a health and wellness consultant, for a women's health spa in Denver, Colorado. I was newly married, ambitious and hungry to prove myself. I was extremely excited to be hired to do two things I loved most at the time, working-out and teaching others how to maintain a healthy lifestyle. Right from the start I worked long hours, became proficient at selling spa memberships, progressed to teaching multiple aerobic classes each day and enjoyed coaching individual members to achieve their fitness and nutrition goals. I adored the clientele, the positive environment, and my co-workers, however working twelve-hour days four to five days a week was outrageously hard on my relationship with my new husband.

I was very successful as a spa consultant and was promoted to spa manager within three months. The following year I was asked to take on the role of company sales trainer and that is when my challenges began. I was happy and then I wasn't. I didn't realize until year number three how I had gone from loving everything about my work, to feeling completely drained by it. The long hours and dedication had paid off in promotions and status, but my personal life and soul was suffering. I was tired most days and training others in sales wasn't a passion. Not the same passion I had for teaching health and wellness, nor the rewarding experience of supporting in dividual clients to achieving their personal goals. I was caught in the cycle of achievement for the wrong reasons. It crept into my life by way of boosting my ego and paycheck, but bleeding me of the most important and valuable components of life, my faith, and the relationship with my husband as well as my love of being in service to teach and support others.

    I wish I could say I woke up to this stark and ghastly way of life, but in actuality I stuck it out a few more years, blindly allowing the rat race to abuse me. I am grateful to say when I discovered I was pregnant, a year later, the first thing I did was to re-arrange my schedule so that I had more time for my home life and myself. Thinking back, I do not remember asking if I was on the right track, I was just going full out without regard for my truth and my future family. However, with motherhood encroaching, I finally started to realize all the joy I was missing in my life and began praying and affirming change for the better.

    Our son was born in December of 1986 and the world with all its demands faded into the background as I discovered the beauty, grace, and challenges of motherhood. With my new infant, came the sparkle and joy of faith, which I had pushed aside for money and endless hours of work. I managed to negotiate a part-time schedule at work while balancing full-time motherhood; it was a blessing for a few months, but my supervisor was anxious to get me back fulltime as business was supposedly floundering in my absence. Reality hit me hard as I search for trustworthy childcare providers. I prayed to be guided in my search for a safe, caring and reliable soul who I could trust with my precious six-month-old, and God provided. I must say the provision was for me as well, because my perspective had changed as the voice of God spoke loudly to my soul. Changes were in the works as synchronicities were lining up.

WHEN YOU MAKE THE SHIFT

I believe each of us is on earth for the adventure, the joy, the lessons, and to uncover our own mystery. I believe we are more than our physical bodies – for we are eternal spiritual beings having a human experience. I believe that on a grand scale somewhere in the massive universe there exists a hall of records where each life is documented, and significant. However, there isn't a specific road map leading the way in your life, only the record of what has been. The beauty of an open road is the freedom and opportunity it affords. Along with God, we each write your own story and own our truth, creating our own reality.

If there isn't a road map, the question of, *"Am I on the right track?"* has no value. The better question of self-actualization is, "Does what I am doing or how I am living feel *right* and good to me? Is this good for me? Is this good for others concerned? Is this good for God? These questions are the baseline of many of my decisions. If a question passes the three-way test, then it gets a green light to go ahead.

Love gets a green light. I believe a sense of responsibility for one another is placed deep within our heart. We as people are meeting up now on earth to experience and enjoy life and to care for one another. If we have been given any type of roadmap for life, it is simply the street named, "Love". The path of love has multiple meanings and expansive definitions, yet in its purest sense, it is an all-encompassing recognition of oneness with another, better known as compassion.

    Love is simple and complex, it is the essence of humanity and the embodiment of all there is. From birth as a human baby through adulthood and until we return home to the heavens, we are seeded with a mission to love. From self-love to compassion for the masses, we are to explore all manner of this complex emotion in order to fortify our eternal bond. In my example of my first job out of college, it is clear that I was easily lured by money and status, despite its grueling effect. However, with the birth of my first child, I was jolted back into soul alignment and reminded by the strong emotion of –*love*, to do the right thing. I wanted to have more joy in life, and quality time with family and just like that, a new opportunity to work as a director for a large preschool fell into my lap. With my background in education, I was a natural for the position, a bonus to all this was my son and I went to work together daily, during the important early years of his life. New lessons were yet to challenge me, but I was now wise enough to check within regularly and ask, "Do I feel good about what I am doing, and how I am living?" This question and the practice of reflecting and checking with my soul and heart have served me well since that time. I also began to ask my angels for support as well.

THE ABUNDANT GUIDANCE FROM THE ANGELS

Speaking of angels, let's move forward a few decades, past the birth of my daughter in April of 1993, attaining my graduate degree, and past my work as a public high school teacher, to a time when once again I am searching to God, "With -*love* as a mission what am I to do and why?" I prayed. At this point in my life as well as today in present time, I honor a steady practice of meditation where I welcome answers to complex questions in quiet moments with God and the angels. The answer then and now, meets me daily in a continual stream of spiritual awareness. Gone are the days when I choose material gain over relationships and love. However, the best lessons still show up as challenges, and the best days are filled with revelations and unexpected surprises. Seeing the world in this manner is so abundantly fun, as opposed to spinning out of control in worry or anxiety. One synchronistic day occurred shortly after I wrote my first book, on one of my favorite subjects, the *Angels!* But first, let me share a short history about my own early childhood beginnings in Brazil and how my relationship with my beloved angels came to be.

    My connection with angels and the angelic realm began at a very young age. I was born in Brazil to a courageous woman who had her heart set on traveling to America in search of a husband for herself and a father for me. In her absence, I discovered the love and guidance of the angels. I was three years old when mother left me in the loving care of my grandmother and aunt. I didn't know America was 5000 miles away, from Sao Paulo, Brazil, nor did I have a concept of time and the years passing. Under the loving care of my maternal grandmother, I learned to pray and to trust my natural sixth sense. As a devout Catholic, my grandmother dutifully marched me to church every Sunday. We wore lace head coverings, our best dresses, shiny shoes and sat for hours in a grand cathedral filled with faithful followers in prayer, song, and devotion to The Lord.

I was a small child when I first saw the angels. Sitting quietly in the church pew tucked in among hundreds of patrons, I experienced an expansive compassionate emotion and perceived dancing sparks of light around many persons. In that era, the Catholic mass was approximately two hours in length, yet I was often entertained and mesmerized by the lights that amplified with song, and resonated vibrantly with particular prayers. I did not know what to call this phenomenon, for I did not know at the time that others were not able to see and feel the presence of angels. When I mentioned the lights to my grandmother and aunt, they told me, very matter of fact, that it must be the angels of the Lord accompanying us at church.

From that time forward I associated the compassionate sparkles of light; I felt and saw with the angels of the Lord. I was fortunate as a young child; to have hours of quiet playtime and the angels would be in attendance, playing right alongside me. I didn't speak out loud to them, because we communicated through love and emotion. I knew their presence as love, kindness, prayer, warmth, and goodness. Today in present time, I realize the angels were communicating with me through the power of emotion and energy. One might call this wishful thinking or childhood imagination, but for me, I know the angel's presence, they have never left my side and I attribute many of the blessings in my life to the guidance and love I receive from the angelic realm. I wrote and published my first book in 2013, *"Angel Decoding, Secret Keys to Communicating with your Angels"*. I loved writing that book, it was as if the words flowed from me each time I sat down to write and in roughly a year, the book was complete. Being an author has its advantages and shortly after the book was published, I was asked by numerous local libraries to offer a "book talk" and signing to interested patrons. For one of those scheduled book signings, the program director asked if I would demonstrate my work with the angels by offering audience readings and participation. I prayed about this new opportunity and with confidence, gladly obliged.

FOLLOW YOUR HEART AND LIVE YOUR DREAMS

Unbeknownst to me, on the morning of the program, patrons began calling into the library to inquire as to when the doors would be opening for the event, which was to be held later that same evening. We had planned to potentially have an audience of twenty or thirty, however, people began to show up at noon to save seats. When I arrived at six in the evening I could not find a parking space in the lot and had to walk a couple of blocks to enter the building. At the door, I was met by the program director, who looked a bit anxious as she gently told me that a larger audience than we expected had arrived and more chairs were set up to accommodate the overflow.

I was pleased to hear this, however, it did not register with me until I walked in the room that evening to speak, that there were over 300 people present, with standing room only. The front door attendant had begun turning people away due to fire code and safety regulations. I was honored and frozen in fear for a few moments as the brevity of the situation sunk in. I was unexpectedly responsible for entertaining the largest audience I had ever faced for roughly two hours. I was suddenly feeling weak in the knees, not feeling worthy of all this attention. In my inexperience about these things, I had not planned a complete program, only to *go with the flow* of the group's vibe, combined with questions and answers, allowing genuine knowledge regarding angel communication to lead the way. Oh man, was I in for a growth opportunity in action!

From my sudden frozen state of *fear*, I meekly managed to excuse myself to a nearby bathroom and began taking deep cleansing breaths as I patted my face and wrists with cool water. In those few moments before taking the floor to speak, I found the quiet and safe space of "calm" I truly needed to precede and succeed by *praying*.

Prayer is one of the most powerful tools known to man. I love the rhythm and certainty of a rote prayer and the creative authenticity of a heartfelt intentional prayer. In moments when I find myself feeling small, I work up my confidence by reciting "The Our Father" and "The Hail Mary" in a continuum. For several minutes I was lost in the comfort the words have entrained in me and suddenly I was back in church as a young girl in Brazil, with a choir of angels surrounding the congregation. The world was right again. I wasn't alone. The angels in all their glory would hold my hand, whisper in my ear, and encircle the awaiting crowd.

As I made my way to the large hall to speak, I knew I was going to be fine. The presentation before me was not about me, it was about shining the light of hope and support for all the people whom were guided to attend. It was about the grieving mother, hoping to receive a message about her baby who passed away before she could call herself a mother. The presentation was for the little girl who sat on the floor because there wasn't a seat for her that night, and gingerly asked if her Daddy in heaven was okay? The night was for the man who had lost the only person he had lovingly cherished for over forty years, unaware of how difficult life would be without her. This was for them and I was the vehicle for love, for hope for comfort. This presentation would bring joy, and assist me in realizing the gift and reason for living. That evening I was filled with compassion and was propelled by the light of God's angels as I rounded the corner and opened the door to do what I have come to understand as my mission, as my *Truth*; I talk to the angels and somehow they communicate back to me and the miracle of eternal love is witnessed and there is healing for all who are present.

On this journey to our truth we will discover joy by

remembering, that only Love is Real. Thank you for reading. Thank you angels. Thank you life lessons. I send you all love from my heart to yours,
Maria

ACKNOWLEDGMENTS

I am eternally grateful to the many people who have touched my life as teachers, students, clients, and friends. I am ever blessed with a loving family, whose encouragement has left a deep impression in my soul. A special thanks to my dear husband Richard Peth, and my children, Derek and Rachel. All my love!

Maria Peth

Maria Gurney Peth PhD. is a spiritual teacher, angel therapist, intuitive life coach and angel decoding specialist, in high demand for her ability to connect with the angelic realm. Maria has worked with thousands of satisfied clients in personal consulting sessions, life-affirming workshops, as well as local and destination retreats.

People are drawn to Maria's genuine sincerity and natural intuitive abilities. Clients schedule sessions for the magic and leave with solid strategies to support a centered and blessed life. Born in Brazil, yet raised on American soil, Maria believes in living authentically, soulfully, and with purpose. She is a life-empowering spiritual teacher and soul coach. Maria has earned degrees from the Uni versity of Iowa and University of Denver with focus on education and social psychology. She earned her doctorate from the American Institute of Holistic Theology in metaphysics. Maria is a published author, motivational speaker and gifted teacher. She is proud and grateful to be married to the same wonderful friend and partner for more than 37 years.

ABOUT MY BUSINESS

Established in 1999, Maria's Angelic Enlightenment office is located in Waverly, Iowa. However, Maria Peth Phd conducts business anywhere in the world. Her destination retreats to exotic high energy locations have earned her world fame as have her individual angel readings and soul coaching sessions. Please schedule your individual session with Maria, by visiting her website.
www.MariaPeth.com

Website:
www.MariaPeth.com

Facebook:
https://www.facebook.com/Angelic.Enlightenment/messages

Twitter:
@AngelicMaria444

Instagram
AngelicMaria444

THANK YOU!

FREE VIDEO CLASS: Find free recordings of Maria's class, Sacred Circle with Maria on her YouTube channel.

FREE MEDITATION: Also enjoy a free angel meditation when you register for her monthly news letter directly from her website.

RECONFIGURE YOUR COMPASS

Lori Ciaccio

I have a story to tell you that will change your life. Your story won't be mine and that's not what matters. What matters is that all stories belong to all of us; different players, different circumstances and different outcomes. Have you ever heard a story that you thought, I don't relate to that in any way? Or, good god, glad that didn't happen to me? Or, better yet, this isn't even interesting enough to finish reading or listening too? Well, here are my thoughts and wisdom on that subject. DROP THAT NOW! I mean, really? When you feel a push against something in your mind or notice it in your words; that is the answer and that is the connection. If you find that you are having these thoughts, take note: Not interesting: are you telling me that all your stories are interesting and that you are ok with someone thinking that about you? Don't Relate: you must not know anyone… really? Or have you stopped talking and listening to the ones that are surrounding you? Thank God that didn't happen to me… but it did and here's why… every time something happens to anyone it happens to all of us… I know, that this one is TRUTH!

Did you know that if you don't pay attention to your body, it will scream at you eventually?

Did you know that you have a choice to chase things before they chase you?

Did you know that you already have everything you need inside of you?

Here me on these!

Sometimes our story is intertwined with others and it's hard to unwind the complication….

If my story catches your attention, be it the title, or the description, or even the opening chapter; my intention is to tell it in a way that you are aware, as the reader, that you are never alone. This "you are not alone" is a pop culture quote right now, and there are many that will dispute that, however, right now at this time in our history, you have never had more access to others. We have social media, YouTube, online groups, in person groups and everything in between. So all that being said, you may feel alone in the experience that you are having and I hope that my story, if for only one person, touches you in that alone place and that you will never feel that again.

MY STORY, MY WARRIOR MENTALITY... WHEN DID THAT START?

So it all started when I woke up! It was the Spring of 2003. I found myself in Bakersfield, California, fired from a lucrative, mortgage paying corporate job that I detested! I mean the kind of job where going to work every day made you feel like you were either going to vomit or you discovered the actual feeling of gravity pulling you down to the couch. One morning, I was summoned to a hotel lobby, where my boss and his colleague, informed me, with no emotion, that I was being let go. The details were not clear, however, in the end, they became clear. But, why wasn't important. It was the impact it had on me that was so profound. Let's explore that a bit here.

My reaction surprised me. I started to cry. In fact, I started to weep. So, here I find myself, all dressed for work, in a beautiful suit, perfect shoes, makeup, and hair, and I am weeping in a hotel lobby. I was caught off guard and completely shocked. I don't remember much, but here is what I do remember. I said very little, in no way did I feel compelled to ask for clarity or even argue as a response. I found myself in flight mode, you know, the kind where all you want to do is get away? Flight mode was not my usual coping skill either, most of the time, it was common for the fight mode to kick in. This was new for me, as in, I became very aware of my surroundings and I needed to flee. I think I signed something, gave over the keys to my car, called a taxi, and headed home, the whole while crying like an uncontrollable teen who had lost their first love or crashed their beloved car.

I remember sitting on the kid's toy chest in the garage. We had converted it to a shoe bin and it was right outside the door that went into the house through the garage. Sitting there with my head in my hands, looking out onto the street through the open garage door, and thinking; I don't have a car! So now I start crying because I live in my first home, ok, first mortgaged home, and I have no transportation. So I just keep crying and finally get to the point of calling my friend Steph. And here is what I remember about the words in that conversation. Nada! But boy do I remember the actions and feelings.

Stephanie came to my rescue. She immediately drove to my home, sat with me in my garage, didn't ask anything, but let me share. This amazing woman brought me everything I needed at that moment. The love, understanding, empathy, and camaraderie that she showed me was undeniably one of the most compassionate moments I have ever experience in my life. I am forever grateful to this beautiful woman for the way that she showed up that day. Unbeknownst to her, she was a part of my awakening. Oh, and let's talk about the gigantic, overwhelming, and generous gift she brought with her that day. She brought me transportation. I mean seriously, she brought over her family's extra car for me to use. Here were the parameters: Use it until you get your own!

I learned some valuable things about friendship that day. Friends don't keep score, they show up no matter what, they LOVE you and girlfriends can make it all better!

This day, and I mean it only lasted a few hours, was the moment that I awakened. It wasn't like I had a vision or the experience of looking up at the sky and a plane skywriting out the new plan. No, it was more to the tune of being hit in the back of my head with a 2x4 and shaking things right into place. I had clearly been on autopilot. Managing work, kids, and the house had all become just a daily task, with a little fun in-between. This day was the beginning of doing things a new way. My will came back, my drive returned, and my presence was reborn. It happened over a few short hours. I was so clear. Clear that I never wanted to work in a situation where someone else was in charge of my future. Clear that I was just functioning and that is not helpful or joyful for my children. Clear that my health was failing. Just plain CLEAR. And the cool thing about that clarity was that I became present. I became present out of necessity, and presence became my coping skill. Cool, right? The amount of control that I had around employment became real for me this day. One could say that some sense got knocked into me, but I say that it got knocked back into me. I was given a gift that day. That gift was unwavering grit.

Wikipedia describes it as:

> **Grit** *in psychology* is a positive, non-cognitive *trait* based on an individual's *perseverance* of effort combined with the passion for a particular long-term goal or end state (a powerful *motivation* to achieve an objective).

This unwavering grit was exactly what I needed. I

believe that it was there all along, but not something I knew how to access with awareness.

All my "whys" of starting my own business.... Let's expand on that.

Let's face it. I had lost a job that paid the mortgage. I had lost a job that felt like moon boots. I had lost a job that required me to travel for training and inspiration that did not align with my moral code. I had lost a job that required more and more of my time. I had lost a job that sucked my brain.

Losing the job was the beginning of a true career. But, I had to take some time off to let my brain heal. I was burned out! Not just from the job, I was burned out from, pushing to be the best in high school, graduating from college in 3.5 years, studying abroad in college, living with my fiancé, getting married, figuring out a career, getting the career and not being the best, having a baby, then another, staying at home with the baby, working with the baby, marriage failing, divorce, moving houses, moving cities, building a house, dating, children in school, son has learning disabilities, dad gives up custody, depleted my B12 levels to the point of disease... ekkkkk... All of this in less than 10 years!

So I took a sabbatical, all be it a forced one, but one none the less! I really dug in my heels about not going back into the pharmaceutical arena, and not jumping into a sales career that was aggressive and didn't align with my personal ethics. So, honestly, I had no idea what to do, who I was in my work career, how I could make money, I mean... just plain old lost. Unemployment here I come! Thank goodness I was able to get unemployment insur ance for a few months. It, along with credit cards and savings, got me through until I started my business at the end of the year.

This 6 month period was an amazing time for me. You would have thought that I was frantic or worried. Actually... none of that happened! I was home with my babies, ages 5 and 7, we were totally immersed in each other. IT WAS BEAUTIFUL. We were a team, we nick named ourselves the 3 Musketeers and we did everything as a team. I learned so much at this time about who these little people were, what they truly needed from me and most importantly, I learned about my own strengths and priorities. I felt resentful for a while that I would need to go back to work to support this family. I felt resentful for a while that my marriage didn't work and my ex didn't want to share in the responsibility of raising our kiddos. I felt angry for a while at myself! I had always done everything well and right, and I had fallen. Funny, how when you have time, like a sabbatical, you discover that you fell into where you were supposed to be. It doesn't look like that when you land. Landings hurt sometimes! I mean, for me the landing looked like failure, unemployment, shame, loneliness. I mean let's face it: I was an unemployed single mom. YIKES...

If I hadn't had this failure, I would have continued down the path of least resistance and by doing that, I am sure that my fall would have come eventually. Meaning, if I hadn't been fired, I might have self-sabotaged, I might have become ill, I might have not connected with my little peeps... and how DISTRESSING IS THAT! I received the gift of a sabbatical and I accepted the gift. I moved through all my resentment, anger, and pain to a place of creative, intuitive problem-solving. I am creative, I am intuitive and I love solving problems more than anything!

WHY STARTING A BUSINESS WAS THE ANSWER FOR ME AT THE TIME:

I clearly need flexibility for many reasons. Let's name a few: Children in elementary school that needed a mom that could show up at the drop of a hat; Son with serious learning disabilities, that needed more than average attention; Daughter that needed me in unique ways since her brother was taking more time; I was tired and needed to just chill; I was mom and dad, so I needed to have the time freedom to be able to manage this almost impossible task; AND, I really liked to be in control of my time, versus, someone else (employer) being in charge of my time.

    Another reason that I wanted to start a business, was that I wanted to explore my own heartfelt capabilities. Meaning, I really was sure that owning my business would bring me financial freedom and stability in unique ways. Working for a large corporation felt unstable, required time-wasting meeting and discussions, and had an underlying theme that "they" came above all else. If I was the boss and I owned the company, then I was in charge of all the things that drove me nuts. I love to work and be busy, and at the same time, I was discovering that what drives me was very different from what the incentives where at my corporate job. In fact, I believe that I was not working to my full potential when I worked for a large corporation.

So, let's chat about working at your full potential! I have one goal and one goal only… it has been the same for many years and will continue to be the driver in my life until I meet the end! That goal is to maximize my potential.

Maximizing one's potential has been a bit harder than I expected and many things have gotten in the way along the path. When I broke down my potential in the different roles that my life assigned, I learned that I could only maximize in one role at a time. I had to focus on one area for a while before I was able to focus in another. Here's an example: When I entered into my business and started to build it from the ground up, I had to put being the ideal mom on hold. I had to choose the parts of being a mom that were the most impactful, that I could do well and easily, while I was focusing on my company. It was hard and it was possible, but don't get me wrong, it was one of my biggest challenges during those early years. Here are the roles I was unwilling to give up: reading every night, snuggles every day, one on one focus with each child so they could feel mommy being present, and lots and lots of talking! So the following went out the door: organized house, organic cooking, clean clothes making it to the drawers, extracurricular activities, and more… AWWWW the freedom! Sometimes these and other things would start to nag at me in the back of my mind and I had to learn to let them go and be present! When I was present and reminded myself that this was the season we were in, then I was able to work at my maximum potential in that role.

When my company was up and running, then I was able to switch to maximizing my personal potential... mommy! And no surprise, I met my husband at this time, so I got the opportunity to maximize the role of girlfriend, single mom and then wife! Wow... that was a ride. I would have never been able to move into those roles if I was trying to maximize them all at the same time. It took planning and intuition on my part. Intuitively I knew that exact order to go in. I knew that if we didn't have an income, the 3 Musketeers would not be able to have stability, and my ability to recognize this was the beginning of learning the art of maximizing Lori.

I really believed for many years of my life that I could do more than one thing and do them all well. On the contrary, I discovered that this was very far from the truth. I had to learn to slow down and focus on one thing at a time. Now, I don't mean tasks that fill up your day, where you find yourself doing things that don't take a ton of thought. I'm referring to big things: building a business, raising and bringing up children, being a wife, maintaining relationships with family and friends, and self-care! I also discovered that the intensity of my focus was shorter lived than I imagined. So when I focused on BIG... I had to do it fast and furiously so that I could move to a new focus... mix it up to keep me engaged. And instead of feeling bad about this part of my personality, I embraced and acknowledged it! And used it to get tons accomplished...

WHAT IS A KID IN THE CRACK?

Some of you don't need an explanation, some of you might have an inkling, and some of you will give me reasons why they exist and how to fix them. If you don't think this matters to you; you are wrong!

I have spent years raising a son that was not following ANY traditional paths. I was up against conventional thoughts and practices, in medicine, culture, and education. I felt alone in these areas for sure. I had my mom, my friends, a therapist and Special Ed team for support so you might think, oh, she wasn't alone. Alone is a place you feel in your heart. Feeling alone with the doctors, the principle, the teachers and acquaintances was indescribable. Let's face it, we all want to fit the normal path. I was already a single mom, working, "barely hanging in there"; I wanted to feel NORMAL too.

So, people now ask me how did you handle the pressure? How did you feel ok? You always look so put together? Let's talk about that for a bit! And let's talk about what you see is not always what is happening!

Handling the pressure: Let's define the pressure for me. It boiled down to one key element and this is the element we can all relate to. IN THE END, WAS HE GOING TO BE OK? As soon as I was able to embrace the fact that I have absolutely no control over the future, was I able to learn to control all the pressures around me. I constantly asked my self during stressful events: Am I willing to die on this hill? What is the alternate route? I no longer had the option of being stressed, seriously it was getting me nowhere. I found that my worry was leading to distrac tion. To deal with the stress, I was procrastinating, binge-watching TV shows, and reading fantasy fiction. So I decided that Pressure wasn't working for me. It wasn't an easy decision, because let's face it: I could justify TV, Movies, good books, shopping and all the like… But in the end, letting go of Pressure, deciding it wasn't a feeling that I wanted to relate too any longer, gave me ultimate freedom. This freedom leads to NORMAL daily practices and habits. And when you feel NORMAL, everything is OK, and actually, your creative mind kicks in!

Did I feel OK? NO. Let's face it, I didn't feel OK. Daily, I was in an uphill battle. Many people would offer loving advice, like "God won't give you more than you can handle." What! Give me a break, how about some real advice on peaceful dinners, or daily calls from the principle, or pure exhaustion? So here is the bottom line: If you don't take care of you, your body will! I mean this literally. My body took care of my problem. Do you know how it did that? My body decided to be ill! My body, said "enough", if you won't listen to your mind, then I will stop this madness. Here's the list: B12 deficiency… that's quite the story, reduced lung capacity, food allergies, fevers, vomiting, cervical spinal fusion, rashes, and the list goes on and on. Here's the bummer with all of this: it took me years to understand what my body was telling me because I didn't really want to listen to its amazing advice. One day, and it was one day, I be came aware. Today, I can feel when my body is sending me a message, one that I have ignored from my brain, and I heed its warning.

You always look so put together: That's because when I go out in public, I take a shower and dress appropriately. I mean, of course, I always look put together! Don't you dare come to my house though, I mean seriously, I am a sweats, no makeup, braless girl! I have been in a sales career all my working days and I realize that being put together is part of that package. I also learned that in order to be taken more seriously when it came to advocating for my son, I needed to present a certain persona in order to get the results needed. Now, in some ways, this backfired on me, because I appeared to be far more knowledgeable than I was, and my appearance sent the message that I didn't need help. I was stuck in that place for a while. I still believe that this place, you know, the one between a rock and a hard place, is a place where you develop amazing grit and tenacity. The biggest lesson for me in that place was to learn how to present myself with authenticity. When I let down the walls of fear, hopelessness, and appearance, I was able to BE put together, not LOOK put together.

It was all these questions that people asked; how do you handle the pressure, how do you feel ok, how do you look so put together?, that brought me through all the stages of my story. These questions helped me to develop into the person I am now, and the person that I continually evolve to be. This is true for all of us. Sometimes, it's not easy to hear the message, and let alone take ahold of it and develop yourself. If you are thinking or believing that I had it easy because at least people asked…don't kid yourself! You already know inside what the questions are and you already know the answer. The difficulty lies in your ability to put the pieces into the pattern that serves you best in that moment.

How do I arrange all the pieces today?

I wing it! Yes, I do, because that is a place of action and less thought. My intuition kicks in and I often make the best choices here.

If the day is too long and I feel like I am on a hamster wheel, I go back to my old standard for the last 25 years! Make a big bowl of Mac and Cheese, put on my robe and watch movies!

Get on the treadmill or walk in nature. This grounds me in about 30 minutes.

And on the days that it is all too much, like hospital time, or pure anger, I SIMPLY JUST GO TO BED EARLY! Things are always better the next day, and honestly, the sun always comes up no matter what, so I might as well start anew!

When did I notice that I had a kid in the cracks? In hindsight that is so very clear, and at the time, not so much…

Here are some thoughts on what I was noticing at the time. Josh was a high-risk pregnancy in that the first ultrasound showed that he had enlarged ventricles of the brain. This can mean a few things, i.e. hydrocephalus, developmental delays or NOTHING. Keep in mind that this pregnancy was in 1994 and he was born in February of 1995. I was 25 and no risk… so the specialists just monitored me for amniotic fluid levels and took measurements of the brain and body at different week counts. It is my understanding now that we would have received a more definitive diagnosis based on current times. However, this is how things were handled then, especially if you are young, no history and everything else looks normal. I was not a candidate for amniocentesis.

Where was I mentally during this time? Exceptionally excited to be having a baby! Funny how the brain (especially before 26) is looking at the fun and not at all concerned about the outcome. This is the diamond of the story. It is my gift. The gift to be able to key into my intuition and winging it. I would have never chosen abortion or even fear. I chose complete excitement and joy.

I had no idea that I was going to have a kid in the cracks. My pregnancy was the first indicator though. Why, because I was monitored as high risk, he had enlarged ventricles, low amniotic fluid… but by the time I delivered, all appeared normal and there was no immediate follow-up.

Segway here… Let's define what being in the cracks is, or more clearly, what I mean by having a kid in the cracks.

> Someone that appears normal, does something a bit different, but in the end, the result is similar to normal parameters.

Examples include:

Enlarged ventricles but no apparent delays or water on the brain

Crawls, but prefers to roll to places and pick up things with feet, rather than hands, then brings object to the hands.

Took 30 steps at 14 months, landed on bottom and didn't try to walk until 16 months... this is the latest age to walk before concern sets in...

Head circumference is 110 percentile, pediatrician says "never had a kid in the range that was normal", but turns out he is the first for that doctor.

Speech therapy that turns around in 6 months instead of the usual 12 months...

Lazy Eye that never shows up in exams until age 6... able to patch and has full corrected vision in 6 months. Rare!

This child has a lifetime of these types of examples. They cause all sorts of worries for parents, family, some educators, doctors... however the ability to catch up or turn on its own starts to become the norm for that child.

So, let's talk about what this does to me. I'm coping, I'm having another child, I'm learning about advocacy... I feel crazy because my intuition is telling me that something is OFF... I'm getting divorced, I'm a single mom of 2... I'm constantly moving my body and my mind is doing the same. I'm working, I'm not working, I'm starting a side biz, I'm re-entering corporate...

<u>Underneath it all, every step I take is informed, but before I become informed, my intuition kicks in and I start winging it… I am driven by my GUT, ALWAYS. I know that we all have what we need already inside of us.</u>

MESS AND NOT A MESS… truly life! But under all of it, I'm watching and feeling. I am sure I have a boy that is different. He is showing up in ways that I am unfamiliar with, and remember, I have another child, so I am able to see what average development looks like.

I wouldn't say that I was super clear that he was in the cracks until first grade, but looking back it is crystal clear. And when I started to advocate, I was overwhelmed, because I WAS SURE that this was going to last a lifetime, and that scared the shit out of me! Let's be honest, you have this precious baby (waiting for all your life), and he is just as cute as a button, with big eyes, soft skin, I mean… you just kiss them so much, their skin might fall off… JOY!

ADVOCACY?

I'd like to explore how to be an amazing advocate. I'm currently taking a class where I have to ask 10 friends to tell me the 'one thing' they see in me as a strength. It was interesting because different versions of the same answer came up over and over. The one that I thought resonated the most was: dissecting a problem, finding the root of the problem and coming up with solutions; you have the ability to notice things that most wouldn't.

This is true about me and it is why I am an amazing advocate. Here are the areas that I advocate best: medical, educational, your rights (with an attorney's help), and myself.

This is a bit difficult to explain and to explore. Why am I a great advocate? I think it is because I ask excellent and thought out questions. For example: when my son was diagnosed with a learning disability and other health impaired diagnoses, I learned to ask questions and not forget the answers. I wrote everything down and put it in a notebook. This really mattered! Because shortly I found myself having to advocate for his education. No small feat since the school we attended was already biased toward single moms and didn't want the test scores for the school to be affected. Because I asked lots of questions, I learned the following: my child would have to be served in his local neighborhood school, that meds don't work for over 20% of kids, food can make a difference, but not always; I need to have an excellent relationship with the school psychologist, I need to show up significantly more than the average parent, and that there are ways to advocate without being labeled as the difficult parent.

I also became an excellent health advocate! Our medical system will push you through and learning how to advocate for the best health decisions is vital. Here are some of the things I have learned and know to be true: Not all meds work, not all procedures are necessary, you can change your doctor, you can get a second opinion, ALWAYS have someone help you when you are the patient that needs advocacy, there are alternatives that your doctor doesn't tell you about and possibly doesn't know about. It is vital that you ask good questions and keep a notebook or phone with you! For example: I had a cervical spinal fusion; it was rough; one surgeon had a very aggressive plan and the other had a conservative plan. This is difficult to navigate and the pain was becoming a driving force. Questions became vital to the process. Truth be told, I went with the surgeon that could answer specific questions, who had done 1000's of the procedure, was board certified longer and had several patient outcomes to share. And guess what!? He was the man with the conservative plan and now 9 years later, that was an excellent decision on my part! I mean, it is my neck!

Here are my thoughts on how to develop the skill set for advocacy:

> Learn how to self-advocate! This included asking good questions, standing up for yourself, start making good decisions for your own life and getting the support you need from your own tribe.

> Learn to advocate for your child. All children need an advocate in our system today. There will be times that you have to step in for the best interest of your child. Learn to do it without being "that parent" by taking the steps above.

> Learn how to advocate in the medical system. You will find that sometime in your life, you will be going down this path with a loved one, young or old, health doesn't discriminate. Take the steps in #1.

My ability to advocate in our complicated, complex society has changed our outcomes dramatically. Advocacy for me was the ability to take the gifts I already had and to sharpen my skills through learning and putting them into practice.

FINAL THOUGHTS TODAY:

During this entire process, I am building a way of life, a type of philosophy, a way to manage an emerging story.

Following only conventional medicine makes me crazy because it was working only marginally. Following educational guidelines and IEP's, is where I learned about advocacy outside of medicine. Building a support team is a must, but I discovered this is a bumpy road because it is long (lifetime) and most of those around you aren't up for it!

And every day or almost every day, I have some sort of insight that I am able to apply! And every day I feel on some quiet level that I am just winging it because, for me, that becomes the easiest way to breath and be present. I know what to do and winging it with my gut feels more peaceful to me than having a structured plan that fails over and over again.

Permission is granted to do this life the way you need to do it... I GIVE YOU PERMISSION TO do what you already know to do!

ACKNOWLEDGMENTS

To my sweet husband because you always just let me be me. To my courageous son, because you are the definition. To my tenacious daughter, because without you, my life would not have been complete.

Lori Ciaccio

Lori Ciaccio is the owner of Lil Angels Photography in the San Joaquin Valley. She has served as managing director of Polka Dot Powerhouse Fresno chapter for the last 2 years and is currently developing a new company aimed at serving parents with adult children living at home.

Website
loriciaccio.com

Facebook Personal Page
Lori Oden Ciaccio

Twitter
@LoriCiaccio

Instagram
Loriodenciaccio

THANK YOU!

FREE VIDEO CLASS: I have a companion video course on CREATING HARMONY WHEN ADULT CHILDREN LIVE AT HOME.
You can head on over to www.LoriCiaccio.com to sign up for it.

JOURNEY TO UNSTOPPABLE

Jessica Mull

I stood backstage with fourteen of my newest friends, waiting for my name to be called. I could hear the roar of the crowd, over 6,000 strong. I felt nervous and excited.

Thoughts of self-doubt began running through my mind, "Why am I here? They picked the wrong person. What if they see my extra skin, what if they leave while I'm sharing my story? I don't deserve to be here."

It was as if, in my mind, I had transported back to my 252 pound self, instead of the current me that had lost over 100 pounds and was being recognized as an IsaBody Finalist.

At that moment, Eric squeezed my shoulders and Mari, reassuring as always, proclaimed "You've got this,

Jess!" Their support and love helped to clear my head just as Blake called my name. I ran on stage, waving and posing for the crowd and they continued their applause. "Oh my gosh," I thought. "They are cheering for me!"

Blake lifted the microphone signaling the crowd to silence. "Jessica, tell us how important the right mindset was for you to reach your goals?"

I began to speak from my heart. "This past year, I discovered a lot about myself, and disappointingly, I didn't love myself."

I felt a lump in my chest as the tears threatened to fall. Admitting to 6,000 people that I didn't love myself was hard, but it was my truth. I knew someone in the audience needed to hear my story. I took a deep breath and continued.

"I knew I had to change that. I was so tired of being told how I should be living my life just because of labels. Even after losing all that weight, something still wasn't right. I realized my mindset had to catch up to my transformation. My weight had gotten so out of control. I was destroying my body to the point where I couldn't put any weight on my feet. In my mind, I thought, 'you have to be kidding me!' I was blessed with an amazing, adorable rainbow baby and I had to ask myself, what kind of mother would I be? I had envisioned such an active life with my family but I needed a way to make it a reality. I wanted to look into the mirror and be proud of my reflection. I may never be the girl with six-pack abs, and I'm ok with that. I worked hard to be where I am. As long as I am living the healthiest version of myself, the only limits I have set are the ones I decide. I have decided I am limitless and I am unstoppable!"

The adrenaline rush I felt stepping off that stage is a feeling I will never forget. I was so moved by the idea that sharing my story could inspire others.

I remembered watching episodes of The Biggest Loser and dreaming of the chance to not only inspire people, but to be the person that no longer had to yo-yo diet.

Now, here I was, an Isabody Finalist, having lost more than half my body weight. I realized at that moment that it was no longer about me. I had done the work. I transformed my body and my mind. Now, it was time to lead and inspire others to live a healthy lifestyle. It was time to share more of my story. It was time to share the pain and experiences that caused me to reach my highest weight of 252.2 pounds. It was time to share what I did to lose over half my body weight. It was time to share the tools I used to shed the mindset that kept me trapped in a body that I didn't love.

Most of all, it was time to trust that I wouldn't sabotage myself in the process. It was time to trust that my power to help others comes from my ability to love myself.

BULLIED

I was an active child and young adult. I loved playing sports and being outside. I still do. I grew up in a loving home with a supportive family. From the outside looking in, things were perfect.

But I was bullied. The pain from these early experiences got rooted down into my subconscious, ruling most of my adult life.

In elementary school I transferred from private to public school. At the time, I thought it was the worst decision ever. There were positive things that happened including friendships made, warm memories created, and receiving a great education. But what I remember most happened when I was an innocent 4th grader.

It was my first day of school. I was nervous and thought that the way to make friends would be to bring a big jean purse filled with candy to share. Little did I know that the other kids would think I was trying to "buy" my friends. In my mind, I was just being a good person. I just wanted people to like me. I wanted to fit in and make friends. Instead, I was made fun of. That was the beginning of bullying.

My family worked hard and lived a comfortable lifestyle. Kids assumed that my family had more money than others so we must be different. I was teased because of my frizzy hair and big boobs. Even the girl that ironically would become one of my best friends from high school threw Swedish fish into my hair, thinking it was hilarious.

Every time I was bullied, my heart broke a little. At that age, I had no idea on how these experiences from my childhood would affect me in my adult life. I became an insecure people-pleaser who always apologized, even for things I had nothing to do with. I never felt good enough. I was always trying to be better.

In 7th grade, I made friends with two girls. The three of us were inseparable. One day we were at my house playing and I left them to go to the bathroom. I came back to an empty bedroom and then watched out my window as they ran away, bikes in tow, laughing.

For the rest of that year, they "tortured" me. It was so hurtful that I even asked my parents to transfer me to a different school. They looked into it, but nothing changed. I counted the days until summer when I would never have to see them again.

Years later, I had the chance to remind these girls what they did and how it affected me. They barely remembered and were apologetic. But the damage had been done. I had developed abandonment issues and self-sabotaging behaviors. I turned to food for comfort, to numb the pain and insecurity. My thoughts had begun to haunt me, "Would I ever be good enough? Why don't I
have a boyfriend? What's wrong with me?" It got so bad that in 9th grade, I even tried to commit suicide.

GRANDPA JERRY

My grandpa Jerry was one of my favorite people in the world. He died when I was twelve, just six months before my Bat Mitzvah. Jerry never fought with grandma Shirley. He put her up on a pedestal, as he did with all of us, including my mom. He believed in me and made me feel like I was the most special girl in the world. He promised me that he would be at my Bat Mitzvah but in December 1992, he had a heart attack. I had no idea that would be that last time I would ever see him or even speak to him.

When he passed, another part of my heart broke. This was my first experience with death and it felt like he abandoned me. I began to lose trust in people that I was close to. I still miss him so much. I am reminded of him every day as I look at my son. I keep a picture on my desk of Grandpa Jerry touching the wall in Jerusalem. Some day, I will touch that wall just like he did. In my mind, it will be the exact same place and our hands would be touching.

YO-YO DIETING

My weight was another source of ridicule. At an early age I compared myself to everyone. I thought, "If I am thinner, people will like me. Life will be easy."

In my junior year of high school, I stopped eating. Thankfully I had great friends who brought their concerns to an adult. But before I was confronted, I passed out at a lacrosse game. I ended up on a golf cart with the sports trainer, being fed a Nutri-Grain® bar. Isn't it funny the details we remember? I remember the trainer because I had a crush on him.

Fortunately, that was the end of one downward spiral. Starving myself was not the way I wanted to live. But it was the beginning of a long road on the diet yo-yo and obsessing over my weight. I tried everything including pills and fad diets. You name it, I tried it.

I went off to college in a new city, but the patterns were still the same. Just like in high school, all of my closest friends were gorgeous with beautiful bodies. I compared myself to them and did not understand why I couldn't be more like them. I'm not blaming others as much as I'm recognizing that this was a habit I created in my thinking. My mindset was corrupt, and I didn't know there was a different way to live.

I exercised a lot in college, often biking around the monuments in Washington D.C. Even though I could ride 26 miles a day, I still gained weight. And then lost it, and gained it back again. It was always a roller coaster for me where the number on the scale was my focus and food was always on my mind. As a normal college kid, I drank a lot of alcohol. This didn't help my weight, and when I graduated, I was heavier than when I started.

LIMITLESS

In my early twenties, I embarked on the adventure of a lifetime. I spent 100 days at sea. I met incredible people and made lifelong friends while studying the history, culture, and traditions of people everywhere.

Semester at Sea was not just any study abroad program. It was a time of pure self-discovery combined with helping others. As we traveled to multiple countries and continents, I quickly realized how fortunate I am. Circling the globe was an extraordinary experience that not many can say they have had.

Semester at Sea taught me that the only limits I have are the ones I set myself. To this day, I still remember being in the middle of the Pacific Ocean, traveling from Vancouver to Japan, with no land in sight. It made me feel anything was possible.

Somewhere along the line, I lost sight of the adventurous, limitless, unstoppable girl I had once been.

Perhaps it was the pressure after college to follow the "American Dream."

I got a job but soon realized I was not cut out for the typical 9-5 schedule. I needed flexibility, so in 2005, I started my own business. Despite my months at sea, I fell back into the "real world," and began living the way I thought I was supposed to live.

After college, it was just one "DIET" program after another. I would lose weight with one, gain it back, and then repeat. It was a vicious cycle that I never thought would end. I know I'm not alone, as many of my girlfriends have gone through this same cycle. It took until I was 35 to learn that it all comes down to MINDSET and really good nutrition. But there would be a few more setbacks and miracles before I got there.

ILLNESS

In 2005 I was diagnosed with mononucleosis. Things that were once dormant in my body came alive with vengeance. My parents work in the medical field. One crazy winter I told them my toes were abnormally cold. There didn't seem to be anything medically wrong with me, so I bought a pair of Ugg sheepskin boots. But no matter how many pairs of Uggs I bought, my feet were still so cold. Something wasn't right.

What came next was a slew of doctors and specialists that diagnosed me with anything from Lupus to Raynaud's Disease. But none of them were right. It wasn't until 2008, when I had my first DVT (blood clot), that I was officially diagnosed with an autoimmune disorder called Antiphospholipid Antibody Syndrome. Eventually they would add celiac and fibromyalgia to the list.

I was very fortunate enough to have a father who wouldn't give up on. He researched and got me appointments with some of the best doctors in the world. To this day, my dad still has an excel sheet with my blood work from the beginning to current. I don't even want to think what could have happened if I didn't have him.

It was around this time that my husband Dan and I were trying to conceive our first child. Unfortunately, we learned that one of the main "side effects" of this disorder was miscarriage.

This news was devastating. I went into online groups for support, only to be to be told I was selfish to even think of getting pregnant. I knew I needed to stay positive and yet all I experienced was negativity and misery. I eventually left the group, more determined than ever to not let this disease define me.

LOSING LILLY

We eventually did conceive. Our baby girl, Lilly, was due in the Spring of 2010. My pregnancy was anything but easy and that year was one of hardest of our lives.

I was in the hospital nearly every week, sometimes multiple visits. A few times I was rushed to the ER. The doctors could not determine if my difficulties were due to my blood disorder.

Dan and I would not give up hope. But a few months

into my pregnancy, they discovered that I had a rare allergy to the injected blood thinner they used. They switched the medicine immediately, but it was too late.

On December 14, 2009, my husband and I went to the hospital, laptops in hand. We joked that this was our new norm. It was second nature for us both to continue working through the testing.

That was the day that we lost Lilly.

No one knows what happened or why. I've been told I was the .000001% because everything that happened to me is very rare. Knowing this didn't help ease the pain of miscarriage that would last for years to come.

THE MIRACLE OF JACOB

After we lost our baby girl, I was very sick. I spent quite a bit of time in the hospital. I was on steroids for months and had several infusions. My mom went to every single medical appointment with me. I cherish her support. My platelets were so low, I was close to death, but the doctors could not figure out how to raise them. Massive amounts of steroids caused me to gain weight and develop a hump on my upper back.

After trying several things, my hematologist Dr. Pickens got creative. I now call him my miracle doctor because as a result, my platelets have not gone below 300,000. To me, this was the difference between near death and life. My body may have been badly bruised from all the procedures, however not worrying about my platelet count meant freedom, it meant life. I am so grateful to the man that saved my life. Because of him, I no longer have the hump, nor do I worry about dying every hour of every day.

My team of doctors told me having another baby would kill me. It wasn't getting pregnant that was the risk, but carrying a child.

But Dan and I weren't ready to give up. We looked into surrogacy and adoption, but my heart wasn't in it. The costs were outrageous. I still don't understand how rescuing a child and providing a loving, supportive home for a child in need should cost so much.

My maternal instinct longed for a child. I trusted my body and myself, knowing it was stronger than anyone knew. Many of my doctors would not support my decision to get pregnant, so I went in search of doctors who would. I found several who believed in me. They planned everything, working together to keep me safe so that I would be able to have my miracle child.

My hematologist called me UNSTOPPABLE, which still resonates with me today.

The first step in preparing to carry a child was to get healthy. I needed to get off steroids and lose the weight I had gained carrying Lilly. I found yet another DIET and began depriving my body of nutrients in order to lose weight. It worked, as the weight came off, at least temporarily.

And, we got pregnant. My doctors watched over me with care and on April 13, 2013, we had our miracle, rainbow baby boy, Jacob.

HUG YOUR LITTLE ONES

During my pregnancy with Jacob, I gained back all the weight I had lost and more. Many people talked to me about diets and weight loss and transforming my body. No one ever mentioned changing my mindset.

My son was born healthy. Soon after, I jumped onto another diet train. A friend and I exercised daily at a local gym. I own my own business so I was able to work from home for the first two and a half years of Jacob's life. Every day, Jacob went to the gym daycare while I worked out. I lost about 30 pounds.

One day, I was working out on one of the cardiovascular machines. My friend had left, so I started scrolling through Facebook. Yes, back then, I was focused on my phone more than my workout.

I came across a post about a woman whose house burned down, her child inside. The message was to hug and kiss your little ones and be grateful. I immediately thought of Jacob. I headed to the daycare room to hold my son and smother him with love and affection.

What happened next was unimaginable. I walked into the big room and the daycare girl was feeding a baby. I remember thinking that was strange, because it's against the rules. She was sitting with two other children. I did not see Jacob and when I asked, she had no idea where he was. I frantically looked around, but he was not there.

I felt my anxiety kick in as I began to panic. Where could he possibly be?

Thankfully, my "mama bear" ears tuned out the sound of the music and the television and tuned into my son's crying. I quickly opened the heavy wooden door to the bathroom nearby. There was Jacob, screaming at the top of his lungs, sitting in several inches of water. He jumped on me like a koala. I will never forget that look in his eyes nor the fear in my own heart, knowing it only takes minutes to drown in a few inches of water. I still don't know how my 11-month-old son got into the bathroom, behind that heavy door. He may be amazing, but that is just baffling.

I WAS A MESS

I didn't get to 252 pounds because of what happened to my son at the gym. But another piece of my heart broke that day. I tried to help the gym improve so that this would never happen to another family again but they just weren't open to my suggestions or concerns.

I tried other gyms that had daycare centers but every time I dropped Jacob off, I would end up checking on him every five minutes.

My husband and I become overprotective "helicopter parents," trusting no one outside of family. I was a mess and eventually gave up. It hurt too much. I told myself I would work out at home, but at this point, all I could think was "It's no use. I've let myself go. What's the point?"

ROCK BOTTOM: MY HIGHEST WEIGHT

I spiraled so far out of control that my weight reached an all time high of 252.2lbs. I was miserable. I love photographs but I began hiding behind people and offering to be behind the camera instead of in front of it. I was embarrassed at my size. I'm ashamed to admit that I even doctored photos before posting them on social media to make me appear smaller, even though I still looked overweight.

On the outside, I was still trying to present myself as happy, outgoing, and filled with energy. But I was exhausted. I had trouble walking, due to pain in my feet. I will never forget the day that I woke up and I couldn't put any weight on my feet. Can you imagine, not being able to walk? I went to a podiatrist and was diagnosed with severe plantar fasciitis. His advice was go to physical therapy, buy special shoes in addition to my orthotics, and lose weight.

This was another devastating setback. I had no idea how unhealthy I had become. When I looked in the mirror, no matter how awful I felt, I could not remember ever being so overweight or unhappy.

My thoughts turned to my family. How was I going to play with my son, take him places, and be the parent I dreamed of being? I was a shell of a person. I felt dead inside. I avoided mirrors because I couldn't stand to see my reflection. What happened to me? I was unstoppable when it came to having my son. I dreamed, wished, and prayed for him. He deserved so much better. My husband and family deserved better. I deserved better.

IT'S ALL ABOUT NUTRITION

On November 15, 2015, I said yes.

I said yes to the adventurous, limitless, unstoppable girl I remembered that was hidden away beneath layers of hurt and years of frustration. I said yes to believing in miracles.

I had no idea what to expect, but I knew I needed to change. The nutritional rebalancing program my friend suggested sounded promising, but I had my doubts. After all, I had tried so many diet plans in the past. This one came with a 100% money back guarantee. I hoped it would be different.

I started feeding myself this superior nutrition, and a miracle happened: my weight began to drop. I say miracle because at this time, I could not work out due to the severity of plantar fasciitis. I learned that health and weight loss is 80% nutrition and 20% fitness. I learned that our bodies can become toxic but we can do something about it. The speed of my weight loss was not typical. I was very strict. I did cheat occasionally, and the weight still came off.

My First "Before and After" Photo

Six months after starting my nutritional rebalancing program, I shared my first "before and after" photo of myself on Facebook. The photos were both taken at the Juvenile Diabetes Research Foundation (JDRF) Charity Gala, one year apart.

I had released 85 pounds.

Posting those photos was hard, and at the same time, empowering. I received so much encouragement. It gave me the accountability I needed to keep going.

100 POUND CLUB

On July 27, 2016, I had lost 100 pounds. I shared my excitement and achievement with the Facebook world:

Soon after, I was privileged to walk the stage in front of over 15,000 people, officially part of the 100-Pound Club in the health and wellness company I partner with.

At first, I had to be nudged. But the stage director was so kind and supportive. He reminded me, "You did this. This is your moment."

I will never forget that first stage walk. There was such an adrenaline rush filled with pride over my hard work at releasing 100 pounds. And I knew, this was only the beginning of something incredible.

MINDSET IS KEY, PEOPLE!

I was still on a high when I returned home from that event. I also felt stuck and unfocused. Old habits were kicking in and I was struggling to maintain my weight, let alone lose more. And my new goal was to lose half my body weight.

I knew it was time to do some self reflection and analysis. To move forward, I had to look back and find the patterns and behaviors that would help me discover why I sabotage my own success. There was no way I was going back to that girl in my before photo. I had to rediscover #unstoppable #limitless Jess.

If one were to photograph my life, it would look like a rollercoaster of different sizes and emotions. Like most people, I experienced challenges, disappointment, loss, and even trauma.

But there were also adventures, victories, and miracles that are worth celebrating. I had a wonderful childhood. I did very well in school. I had lots of friends. I played sports. I was outgoing. I went to a prestigious college, George Washington University, where I graduated with a Bachelor in Fine Arts Degree in Graphic Design.

I have an amazing, supportive family. I have a hus

band who loves and understands me and knows exactly what to say to help me when I'm struggling. Even when I don't listen, he persists until he gets through to me.

I have a son who adores me.

I have amazing parents that taught me to be strong, to be a good person, and many other important life values. Being a parent myself, I know how much we want to protect our children, but we can only control so much. They did their best and I am so grateful to them.

From the outside looking in, my life looked perfect. On the inside, I was hurting. And while there is no one to blame, I wanted to know the root cause for my destructive patterns. I wanted to know how a healthy happy girl who once felt limitless and whose doctor called unstoppable got to be 252 pounds.

Growing up with general anxiety disorder and clinical depression made things difficult throughout my life. I was extremely sensitive and very quick to try and please people. Food was always my go to when things got hard.

Overeating was the only thing that made me feel even remotely complete. Once I started eating in excess, in my mind, I felt like I had already cheated. Why not keep going? That was my mindset.

When the binge eating kicked in, I would eat so much that I couldn't even taste the food. Then I'd get sick. I tried every diet imaginable. I'd lose weight, but when it came time for maintenance, I would self sabotage. My life and my weight would spiral out of control.

When I was dieting, I could not receive a compliment. If someone said I looked good, I somehow translated that to mean it was ok to binge eat again. I had no concept of balance or a healthy lifestyle. While I had become an expert at getting my body to transform, my mind had some catching up to do.

It was my mindset that was causing me to self sabotage.

Fortunately, the nutritional rebalancing system I was having success with had a partner program called Healthy Mind and Body. I was already learning to eat healthy and not starve myself. My body had released toxins and I knew I was feeding myself great nutrition. I was feeling amazing. So I dove into this 60 day program.

I learned that it's human nature to focus on the negative experiences in our life. Mine included bullying, abandonment, and broken trust which led to a lifetime of people-pleasing, self-sabotage, and weight gain, along with turning to food for comfort. I apologize often, even for things that are out of my control or I have nothing to do with. These issues were rooted in my subconscious.

Not only did people let me down, but due to my illnesses, I felt my body had let me down.

These were all strongholds in my mind that I would have to break if I wanted to continue to succeed.

One section talked about setting a fitness goal. I always "watched" people on facebook post about running 5Ks and getting medals. I could never really run long distances, so I made my goal to run my first 5k. I used the app Couch to 5k and slowly built up my stamina. In Fall 2016, I ran my first 5K- Rock n Roll Philadelphia. I beat my own PR by a few minutes! The best part was my husband, son and best friend Ashley were there to watch me cross the finish line. I accomplished something that I always told myself I just couldn't do it. There goes that mind playing tricks on you!

I continued with my Healthy Mind and Body training, and read everything I could about mindset. The book that had the biggest impact on me was called Find Your Why, by Simon Sinek.

During one particular exercise, my mentor Kamie Lehmann pushed me to dig deep to the root of my problem.

I discovered I was lacking in self-love.

It was hard to admit, but I knew it was true. My priority had always been to make others feel loved and accepted, sometimes to the detriment of myself.

I began to see that the extra weight I carried was an attempt to protect myself due to the things that had happened to me as a teenager and young adult. It was as if I was had built an invisible wall of protection around my heart. A wall that was not serving me or the people I cared about.

I knew to break down the wall, I had to learn to love myself.

Letting go of the self-sabotaging issues buried deep in my subscious is still not easy. But it is possible. It takes daily effort and intention. These things don't go away overnight. My mind transformation is still catching up with my body transformation.

I now shop for small and extra-small clothing.
While I'm excited to be in that area of the store, I still catch myself thinking that people are looking at me, judging me, believing I don't belong.

There are times I look in the mirror and still see that

252 pound girl. Learning to love myself means learning to love the past me as much as I love the future me.

I take a lot of deep breaths and correct my mindset often. I catch myself when I automatically apologize for no reason. I choose to live in gratitude for how far I've come. I've worked hard. I deserve to feel good in my body and my life. I choose to break the cycle of my past and leave it behind.

Every morning I wake up and choose to let shit go. I chose to live in the present. I have recently learned to question my thoughts especially when they were not serving me. This gave me the ability to fall right back into living in the present.

I continue to devote time and effort toward my mindset. I am always growing and improving. As I feed my body and mind the proper nutrients, I gain freedom. Freedom to be me and to transform into someone who truly loves themselves!

HALF MY BODY WEIGHT

With the mindset work I was practicing daily, I knew that 2018 was going to be my year. January 1st came and I bulldozed through my weight loss plateau. I refocused on new goals.

I signed up for a 30 Day Macro Challenge. With my increase in workouts, I was not eating enough, a common dilemma for people trying to lose weight and the reason why I was always hungry. The first few weeks of the macro challenge I was so confused, I considered quitting.

But I stuck with it and by week four, I was hooked. I incorporated the superfood nutrition I was already eating and many new foods. I was able to eat foods that I had not eaten in years. Finally, I found balance in my diet.

My new goal was to lose half my body weight. A requirement of the 100-pound club is to check-in annually. My next check-in date was May 1, 2018 and my goal was 126.1 pounds, half of my original body weight.

On April 30th, 2018, I hit my goal!

It felt amazing to share this news with loved ones. It was a huge, life changing achievement. Here is what I shared with my Facebook community:

> *"Tomorrow is officially the annual check-in for my company's 100-pound club. I had a new goal in mind after plateauing for a year & half with my weight loss. At first, it seemed crazy. Until suddenly, it didn't! So I made the decision that in 2018 it was time to break through. I went all in! There was no if, ands or buts!!! When I was able to break through the block in my mind, the weight loss decided it was time!*
>
> *And oh! Did life take me thru the ringer and challenge me!*
>
> *But today - the day BEFORE check in - I HIT my goal! I lost HALF MY ORIGINAL BODY WEIGHT of 126.1 pounds! I won't lie - this last leg took a lot! Bc so much, as I have said before, is about mindset!*
>
> *So I'm here to tell you - don't ever give up! Things are going to slap us in the face - life is going to happen no matter what! Just keep pushing through!!*

Now my next goal when the Drs give me the ok from my arm injuries is to tone up... I've never really focused just on that and not weight loss - so it will be a huge life learning lesson but I am excited for my next phase of my transformation!!!
#isabody #unstoppable #warrior"

IT'S MORE THAN JUST WEIGHT LOSS

I share a lot of before and after pictures on social media. Each person has an incredible story. What's even more exciting is that their health is not the only aspect that this journey affected. A healthy lifestyle is so much more than what most think it is. When you feel good about yourself, the stars start to align.

This journey is for life, body, mind, and soul. I live my life on my own terms. The only limits are the ones that I set, which are none. I feel that limitless mindset that I had in my twenties when I was on Semester at Sea.

My own transformation was about more than just weight loss. There have been so many side benefits and non-scale victories (NSVs). Thank gosh I said yes! I am forever grateful for the nutritional lifestyle that I live by every day.

Perhaps the most significant change to me is that I can now receive compliments with ease. I simply smile and respond "thank you."

I strive to not turn to food for comfort when I'm stressed or upset. Because of the mindset work, I no longer spiral downward when life throws me a curveball. I thrive!

I cannot make medical claims. I still have symptoms from my autoimmune disease (celiac and fibromyalgia). I was diagnosed with both prior to my transformation. These symptoms can include brain fog, chronic pain, and short-term memory loss, just to name a few. But I FEEL amazing!

My body is resilient. Despite the toxicity from processed foods, diet coke and all the horrible stuff I ate plus the stress of dieting and deprivation, it bounced back. I had no idea how good I could feel until I felt it. I feel beyond amazing. I can't imagine feeling any other way!

Despite the challenges from my illness, my recent blood work was as close to normal as possible, while still having the diseases. This is significant: for the first time in my life, I was able to get standard-rate life insurance.

This is such a testament to the company I work with and the nutritional rebalancing products I use.

I am living my healthiest life. I follow up with my hematologist twice a year. My appointments are now completely different from the first few years when I saw him. There used to be a lot of tears and frustration. Now, he's talking about how my story needs to be published in medical journals to show the importance of nutrition and the biome (gut) in improving (not curing) autoimmunes. This, from the man who named me unstoppable many years ago. He truly is a huge reason to why I am unstoppable! He never gave up on me and was open to trying new things. Because of him, I was able to go from very sick to extremely healthy.

Thank you, Dr. Pickens for another great appointment. I can't wait to read the article. #unstoppable #apsawareness #autoimmunes #nutritioniskey

In December of 2018, I was chosen to be an ISABODY Finalist in the company I partner with. This goal was on my vision board. Receiving that call from corporate was something I will never forget. I was one of fifteen chosen out of over 46,000. I won cash, free tickets to annual events, and free airfare and hotel to Phoenix for our New Years Kick Off event, where there were photo and video shoots, interviews, welcome dinners, and more! It was a thrill to share my story on stage.

All the finalists won an all expense paid trip to Costa Rica for two at an all-inclusive resort. That experience meant so much more to me than the prizes. It was a new chapter in my journey. And this was only the beginning.

Because of the experience of being an Isabody Finalist, I gained friendship. Throughout the events, activities, and especially the trip to Costa Rica, I got the chance to bond with the other 14 amazing finalists who quickly became friends.

Most of all I gained confidence. Here is what I shared on Facebook, hoping to inspire others:

> *"Raw and real- Yesterday at the camelback shoot something incredible happened!!*
>
> *Everyone knows how hard I worked my butt of to get where I am! All 15 of us finalists have! To stand with half of the finalists at the photoshoot who have such gorgeous bodies- I'm not going to lie... it caused some self doubt!*
>
> *There was no way I was taking off my tank and just being in a sports bra! Not next to these defined in credible new best friends!*

Then my amazing friends and finalists Lydia Hunt and Mari Weisman persuaded- like a hard persuasion to take off my shirt! Everything was incredible and perfect for this picture... and I said you know what?

This is me! This is who I am! And I'm proud of it and I took off my tank - these photos weren't just any photos! They were corporate! I am so glad I let go of that insecurity and was just me! I had to stop comparing myself to everyone else! Like I said! This is me, this is my story, and my skin is part of all of it.

When fear comes running at you- don't run away- run straight at it and break through! This was a big moment for me! It was right then and there that all the anxiety and lack of sleep this past month just kind of went away with the wind! And now I feel on top of the world! I'm so excited for today's interview and everything to come!! Thank you all! I love you!"
#unstoppable #2019isabodyfinalist #rawandreal

You set your own limits... I decided a long time ago in order to be unstoppable, I had to be limitless!!!

I gained an amazing accountability and support network. Food addiction and overeating are no joke. I am a stress eater. During my journey I learned to not turn to food for comfort. But by no means am I perfect. I may fall, but I am surrounded by the most amazing family, friends, and teammates who support me and raise me up. They remind me how far I have come when I forget.

I have a strong mindset. I can handle a setback or disappointment and I no longer get derailed.

After I hit my goal, doors started to open up for me. I received an opportunity to submit my story to PEOPLE magazine for losing half my body weight. I couldn't believe this. Me? I knew my story was good but PEOPLE Magazine? What an honor.

At 8 am every morning, I did a daily affirmation: I WILL BE IN PEOPLE MAGAZINE. I wanted this. I posted my affirmation big and bold on my vision board. I envisioned the photo shoot where they do a makeover in NYC.

Unfortunately, I was not selected. But I can submit again. From the beginning, I accepted the idea that whether I was in the magazine or not, it was not going to break me. In the past, it would have.

I love myself. At 1/2 my body weight, I got my life back. I can do more than I ever thought my body would be able to do. I never thought my future would be with health and wellness but now I get to help people become the healthiest version of themselves.

Lastly, with the amazing support of my loving husband, incredible family, and friends, my son will never know a fat mom.

LESSONS LEARNED

This weight loss journey has completely changed the trajectory of my life. Here are a few of the lessons I learned and the tools I still use to keep myself on track toward my goals.

Know your why.
People asked me what drove me and I said MY WHY. You have to know what inspires you and motivates you to keep going when you are ready to quit. For me, that's my son. A child's memory starts to form at age three. My son was two and a half at the beginning of my journey. I did NOT want him to know a fat mom. Now when he sees pictures he doesn't ever remember me being overweight and unhealthy. He remembers who I am today. He knows mommy is on a mission to improve people's health, mindset and so much more! He is my why.

Feed your body good nutrition.
There were difficult times when I felt that my nutrition was the only constant in my life. It was one of the few things I could count on even when I felt the earth was falling out beneath me.

Keep learning and growing.
I'm proud to be in network marketing. It is an industry that promotes personal development and lifelong learning. I get paid to earn as I learn. I get paid to lose weight, transform, inspire others, and

become my best self. The best part, I don't gain financial success without helping a lot of other people.

Strengthen your mindset.
I would not be able to maintain my healthy body and life without a healthy mind. Because of the work I've done to strengthen my mindset, I can trust that even when there are setbacks in life, they won't derail me. I won't spiral downward into bad habits.

Focus on the positive.
Everyone's life is filled with both positive and negative experiences. Don't get stuck on the negative. A daily practice of gratitude can help you to focus on the victories, miracles, and amazing experiences.

Share your story and become the teacher.
I am unique. There are people in the world that need to hear my story, because there's something about me that will inspire them like no one else can. As I share my story, I become the teacher, and that keeps me accountable to keep growing and learning. When people are scared and vulnerable, I can share my story so they know they are not alone.

I love me.
I am proud of where I've been and all my body has been through. I also know that I can't do so much for everyone else and nothing for myself.

Set goals and keep setting them.
With every goal I reach, I set a new one. I have a vision board so I can see where I'm going. I affirm what I want and I live with intention and persistence.

Don't ever give up.
So many people fail and give up, but part of success is many failures. When you feel at your complete edge, don't give up, that's the moment when change occurs. Be patient and keep working hard. If you want to change, make it happen. I know change is hard. It's damn hard. But if you want it bad enough, figure it out.

Create a strong support system.
I have an amazing family, supportive husband, and son who adores me. I have friends I interact with daily who call me on my shit. They may allow me to vent, but they are quick to help me turn it around toward something positive. And I'm part of an IsaBody community that inspires me daily to be my best.

I have a choice.
When I started this lifestyle journey, I had no idea what the future held for me. All I wanted to do was lose A LOT of weight. I didn't realize I needed so much more than weight loss and wow, did I get it. This journey gave me life, freedom, and choices. I now see more possibilities than I could have ever imagined. That is my choice.

I have a choice to live a healthy life and focus on the positive. I have a choice to let stress make me cave or simply acknowledge that there is stress in my life and not let it beat me.

I have the choice to accept myself for who I am, where I am at in life, and to be proud of myself.

I choose that everything that I have in my life today is everything that I need and want. We all have a choice. What do you choose?

HOPE FOR YOU

As I write this today, I can truly say I love myself. I can tell you that I am the best version of me both inside and out. My workouts include cardio, weight training. I used to spin a lot but I unfortunately got injured. I still have setbacks like tennis elbow, but I won't let it stop me. I truly am unstoppable.

My latest goal is to tone up and gain more lean muscle mass. My bigger goal is to help others find the healthiest version of themselves, whatever that looks like to them. I may never have 6-pack abs or guns of steel, but I am real. If I can do this, anyone can.

My advice to anyone looking for a big change is to be open to it. Find your why. When you do, hold on tight. Surround yourself with incredible like-minded people that are on a similar journey and will who raise you up. Surround yourself with light and happiness.

JESSICA TODAY

Looking back on my life, I'm in awe. I look at the person I was and how determined I was to change the areas I wasn't happy about. I used to dream of a life where I easily maintained a healthy weight. I am now living that dream and that life. A mindset shift has been key.

Nutritional rebalancing has changed my life. I am the healthiest I have ever been! As I approach my 39th birthday, I feel YEARS younger! I feel capable of things I never imagined were possible.

Thank you to everyone who has supported and cheered me on. Some of you have no idea how your impact has helped me to keep going.

This world is ours for the taking! If you want something bad enough take it! Live it! You deserve it! I know I sure do!!! #unstoppable #3yearshealthyliving #warrior #limitless

#unstoppable

ACKNOWLEDGMENTS

My son Jacob who is and will always be my why. My husband- Dan for calling me on my shit and being by my side! My mom and dad for their support and for giving me the push that I needed to make this change for myself and my family! My "coach" and friend Danielle Groth who stood by my side and kept it real even if I didn't want to hear it! Lori King for helping me make my story flow!! Lastly to my friends, family, and tribe, your support is unmeasurable! You know who you are!

Jessica Mull

Jessica was born November 23, 1980. She grew up with her parents, Bob and Candi, and her older brother, Dan in Springfield, Pennsylvania. In May 2003, Jessica graduated with honors in her major in Fine Arts from The George Washington University and received her BA in Fine Arts. In May 2005, Jessica graduated from The Antonelli Institute (Graphic Arts and Computer Graphics school), which helped further her knowledge of graphic design. She started her own business in 2005 called Jessica Selig Designs. Her focus is on post-production of weddings and events. In the graphic design world she has achieved many milestones and won several awards, including Top album design WPPI. Her true passion is part of her recent journey.

As a transformation coach, Jessica won't ask you to do anything she hasn't already done herself. Her own personal success includes releasing half her body weight! Keeping it off has been her biggest achievement. In 2019, she was selected as a US IsaBody Finalist. She was one of 15 people that were picked out of over 50,000. Jessica thrives on helping others to become the healthiest version of themselves while adding an additional stream of income to their household. In doing so she has been able to triple her Isagenix income over the last three years. Helping people find freedom in their body and bank account is her mission.

ABOUT MY BUSINESS

As a multi-preneuer, Jessica wears many hats, however, her work all centers around helping people look and feel their best. She accomplishes this as a graphic designer doing post-production for weddings and events and as a transformation coach helping people become the healthiest version of themselves. With Unstoppable Transformations - her specialties include weight loss/gain, healthy aging, energy, performance, and financial freedom.

Website
www.unstoppabletransformations.com

Facebook Personal Page
https://www.facebook.com/jsmull

Instagram
Unstoppable_grl

THANK YOU!

FREE health and wellness CONSULTATION: Wanna talk about your health and wellness? Let's do it! www.unstoppabletransformations.com/contact

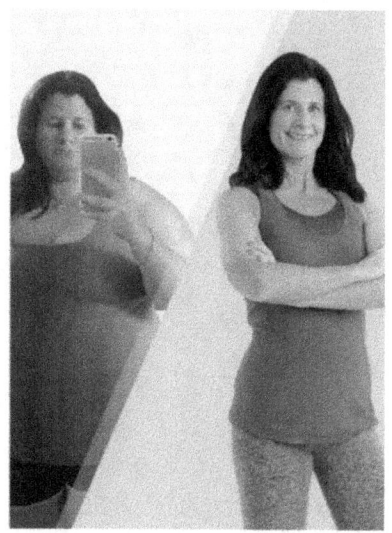

ACKNOWLEDGMENTS

I am deeply grateful of every single woman who added her magic to this book.

This is the fourth book in our Don't Be Invisible Be Fabulous series – and the first book from our new publishing company, Fab Factor Publishing.

My whole-hearted appreciation starts with the readers and supporters of our first, best-selling book; they inspired the second and third and fourth volumes. This journey reinforced in my bones how essential it is to tell stories of real-life women triumphing in their lives. Thousands of women saw themselves in those stories, and then they could imagine a way forward in their own lives. So, of course, Volume 4, featuring more stories of hope and inspiration, had to be born!

Heaps of appreciation also go to the fabulous co-authors from our first, second and third books:

Thank you all!

A whole new conversation.

For those destined for greater.

To reach your next level, let's tap back into who you really are.

An Invitation From Dorris

I'm thrilled you found your way to us!

Right now you may be wondering what your own next steps are to Don't Be Invisible Be Fabulous with your life.

Let start with you stop settling for 'success'.
And start insisting on your FABULOUS work.

I would be honored to have you in our ever expanding circle! Here is a way to be involved:
Get your No Cost image at… BeFabulousImage.com

Dorris Burch

I'm not your average online coach. I don't follow business norms or industry standards. I could give a flying fuck about what the experts say. In the 9 years since I started this business, I have followed my desires, trusted my intuition, and taken the daily inspired action that felt good/made sense to me.

Today, the Fab Factor is a recognizable brand. My job is this: To get you unstuck, to show you how incredibly powerful you are, to move you along your path, to create a space where the beliefs that hold you back don't stand a chance, to teach you to be unavailable for anything less than your soul's desires and destiny, to make sure you know the power of your own creation, and to show you how easy designing a life and business on your fabulous terms gets to be.

I know you have what it takes. I know you can tap into your infinite massive power. I know you have, up until now, only unleashed a fraction of what you are here to do.

I don't shrink, hide, or pretend. I care about delivering women leaders an incredibly fabulous rich and unique experience, which lifts them at a cellular level. But I will be real, kind, and an example for you. If you like the sound of that, then let's do the damn thing.

It's time to design your next chapter.

New Fab You Show Podcast Subscribe today!

We talk about being unapologetic… why?
If you were actually unapologetic about it you'd be doing it differently right now.

Don't miss an episode:
NewFabYouShow.com
Subscribe (it's free) in your favorite podcast app

THE FAB FACTOR
IS THE BRIDGE TO OPEN YOU UP...
BUT REALLY IT'S A VIBRATION THANG.

IT'S ABOUT OWNING WHO YOU ARE IN A WAY TO NO LONGER LIMIT YOURSELF IN WHO YOU CAN BE. YOUR PERMISSION SLIP TO NOT SETTLE FOR A DIMMED DOWN VERSION OF YOURSELF.

IT'S ABOUT HAVING THE COURAGE TO BE MORE OF WHO YOU REALLY ARE AND BE BRAVE ENOUGH TO FIND YOUR FABULOUS AND THEN TO STEP INTO THE LIFE YOU DESERVE.

BORN FOR MORE.
BORN FOR EXCEPTIONAL.
BORN FOR EXTRAORDINARY.
FAB FACTOR ENERGY AND VIBRATION.

Website
TheFabFactor.com

Facebook Personal Page
Dorris Burch

Twitter
@DorrisBurch

Instagram
IAmTheFabulousDorrisBurch

www.ingramcontent.com/pod-product-compliance
Lightning Source LLC
Chambersburg PA
CBHW051400290426
44108CB00015B/2100